DAN DOYLE

DAN DOYLE

The Life and Death of a Wild Rover

Marie Rowan

Black & White Publishing

First published 2007
by Black & White Publishing Ltd
99 Giles Street, Edinburgh EH6 6BZ

2 4 6 8 10 9 7 5 3   08 09 10 11

ISBN 978 1 84502 146 7

Copyright © Marie Rowan 2007

A CIP catalogue record for this book is available
from the British Library

Typeset by GreenGate Publishing Services, Tonbridge, Kent

Printed and bound by Creative Print and Design, Blaina, Wales

Acknowledgements

I am indebted to: Pat Woods for his most generous help in not only allowing me to use his research into Celtic's early history but also for his unfailing interest and support which helped make the writing of this book a pleasure; Maura, Chris and Hugh of the Visitor Centre, Celtic Park, and the irrepressible John Mulvenny; the affable Jack Murray for his photographs of Doyle; my nephews Donald and John Rowan for their enthusiastic interest; Margaret McDonald for happily joining me in a teetotal pub-crawl of Mossend/Bellshill; Paul, Jean and Jennifer Church who encouraged me every step of the way; and Dave Wherry, the ever-generous Grimsby Town FC historian. Finally, my thanks go to Neil Lennon of Celtic FC to whom Dan Doyle would surely have given the nod of approval.

This book is dedicated to my late parents,
John and Isabella Rowan.

Contents

Foreword by Neil Lennon

As Celtic captain, it is especially interesting for me to find out more about one of the first and most inspirational captains our club has ever had. This book has given me the opportunity to discover Daniel Doyle, a very controversial character who thoroughly deserved his reputation as a football maverick. Doyle was a former Lanarkshire miner who saw a chance to escape from the relentless hell of a life down the pit and grabbed it with both hands – but always on his own terms. Joining Celtic gave Doyle much more than rich monetary rewards. As the supporters' favourite son, he enjoyed respect and affection which were deserved and enduring. He led the team by example and always fought till the final whistle blew.

Doyle was a fierce competitor whose intelligent play and uncompromising attitude would be an asset to any modern Celtic side. I challenge any Celtic supporter to read his life story and not feel proud of our wild Irish rover.

Neil Lennon, Celtic FC
Parkhead
2007

Introduction

Celtic Designs

The hurt bit deep and, at the dinner that followed Celtic's 0–2 defeat by Cowlairs in the Exhibition Cup Final on 6 September 1888, John Glass, Celtic FC's president, publicly vowed that the Cowlairs supporters who had so disgracefully tormented the Celtic players that day would be taught a lesson they would never forget. There was only one way to do that. Merely winning trophies would never be enough to satisfy the wearers of the green and white and their supporters. It would be done in the truly unique style of the Celtic race – with ingenuity, skill and passion, the exploits of the Fianna, the legendary heroes of the Celtic tribes of old, transferred to the football field, the players their visible spirit. Nothing less would satisfy the supporters and demonstrate that pride and dignity were the preserve of no one people alone. Not for a moment did it occur to the committeemen that the players who were imbued with such spirit were not available to them. It was part of the Irish psyche and it was Irishmen they wanted. What did not cross their minds was that men of such character were not always easy to handle and, in fact, the individuality that was required actually marked them out as needing an enormous amount of patience and understanding. Also, decisions would have to be made which meant at times the committeemen subordinating their own desire to be 'masters in their own house' for the greater good of the club. In other words, frequent loss of face to get the desired result marked John Glass and his committee as being sublimely pragmatic. But, to the Celtic faithful, that was no problem at all for weren't the players simply supporters incarnate on the pitch?

And far from shying away from the wilder temperamental player, the Celtic committee bought into this idea with a vengeance. They'd been tracking Dan Doyle, the wildest of them all, since he'd played for Hibernian and were hell-bent on securing the services of this man who was rapidly becoming the best left back in Britain. But, that evening, Doyle was still a Grimsby Town FC player.

1

An Opponent Dies

Dan Doyle stood in front of the Grimsby coroner on 14 January 1889 and explained how his challenge which had left Staveley's William Cropper dying had been perfectly fair according to the rules of the game. The coroner's jury agreed and went home for their tea and the Airdrie lad was left to cope with it for the rest of his life. An ex-miner from Rawyards, Doyle had been used to courting death every time he'd gone down the hellhole that was a Scottish pit but this was something else. This was football – a game played for fun. Or was it? Doyle coped for at no time did he play for fun. Streetwise Doyle had packed a lot into his twenty-four years and, fortunately for Celtic, he was destined to do a lot more before he was finished.

A well-known fishing town, Grimsby in Lincolnshire was also noted for its football team. Grimsby Town FC had suited Doyle when he'd joined it in September 1888. Robust was a word which adequately described the method of play employed by both team and new signing. Unfortunately, after Doyle left, the team was shunned by every other team in the area as being too dangerous to play against – a fallacy or an excuse, of course, all stemming from that one tragic incident.

What thoughts were going through Doyle's mind as he and his team-mates walked in silence behind the hearse on its way to the railway station no one will ever know but they can well be imagined. For, although the highly competitive Doyle 'took no prisoners', he was as innocent as he claimed and Cropper's death was a combination of bad luck and the lamentable state of medical expertise in 1889.

The game versus Staveley, a team from Derbyshire, was a friendly and was played in dreadful weather. The pitch was very slippery and a high wind was blowing. Doyle was at left back and, after fifteen minutes or so, he rushed to avert the danger posed to his own goal as Cropper bore down on it, intent on gaining possession of the ball which had been hoisted over the head of Coulbeck, the Grimsby right half. Both men were going at full speed, Doyle's powerful physique being equalled by Cropper's, for a ball which was neither high enough to head nor low enough to kick and, unfortunately, both players came into violent contact.

Doyle's knee struck Cropper's stomach and it was first thought Cropper had only been winded. He was helped from the field to the pavilion and tragically died there the following day in great agony, having been too ill to be moved to the local hospital some two miles away. Cropper had remained conscious for many hours after the collision and at no time did he, his team-mates or any official state that it was anything other than a dreadful accident. The irony of it all was that Cropper, a popular and well-known cricketer who'd played for his county, Derbyshire, hadn't wanted to play as he'd been appointed groundsman at Lord's, cricket's headquarters, the previous day.

Doyle, himself a fine cricketer, was naturally devastated by the death of a young man the same age as himself. At the inquest, Doyle was called on to give evidence and he did so in an honest and forthright manner.

I am a dock labourer residing at Weelsby Street, New Clee, and am a member of Grimsby Football Club. I was in the match against Staveley in the Gardens on Saturday last. The game commenced about twenty minutes past two. I was at my usual post, left full back. Shortly after the game commenced, the ball was passed to Cropper who was on the outside but he did not get it. The ball rebounded from the ground and Cropper ran for it. Both he and myself jumped to breast it at the same time. I caught the ball on the upper part of my right thigh when we collided and Cropper fell. I think I caught his body with my knee. Deceased had given me no provocation to do so intentionally; indeed, it was the first time we had met. Upon Cropper falling, assistance was rendered him and he was helped from the field – by Mr Mason. As far as I am able to say, it was a pure accident. These collisions are not unusual but generally result in a man only being 'winded'. When we sprang into the air, we did so to breast the ball. This is legitimate play for it was too high to kick. I was running at full speed when we met.

After the jury had returned its verdict, death by misadventure, the hearse was taken to the Town station, with the cortège including the Grimsby team which had played in that game a few days previously.

Ironically, William Cropper came from a mining village, as did Doyle, and it was among that community that Doyle, the man for all seasons, felt most at home all his life.

Feelings against the Grimsby Town team in the Sheffield area were to reach such a pitch that Grimsby's two fixtures against Sheffield Wednesday had to be cancelled. But Doyle was a football mercenary and it was probably this more than the grief that he would get from the mindless boo-boys that would make him move from the Mariners.

The directors of Grimsby knew a talent when they saw one. They were quite partial to what they called 'salmon' – Scottish players – and Jimmy Lundie, their Scottish right back who'd been a team-mate of Doyle's at Hibernian in 1887, had been sent to Scotland to do some scouting for them. He 'landed a beauty, no less than Dan Doyle' according to Bob Lincoln in *Reminiscences of Grimsby Town FC.* If Dan had been reading his own publicity, he'd probably have made for the big names as he was earning a reputation as one of the best left backs in Britain.

Altogether, Doyle made four FA Cup appearances for Grimsby, the last on 16 February 1889 against Preston North End (Grimsby losing 2–0), which rather makes nonsense of the belief that he never again played for the club after the Cropper accident. These directors who had stood by him resolutely at the most trying time of his career were reluctant to see him go. But the lure of an extra shilling or two from a league side proved too much for the astute negotiator that was Doyle and he left the scene of the greatest tragedy of his career in July 1889 – not to return permanently to his native Scotland and back down the pit, as had been his first understandable reaction to Cropper's death, but for a brief flirtation with Bolton Wanderers – although the FA have no record of Bolton Wanderers actually registering him as a player – and then quickly on to the great Everton for whom he signed in July 1889, being registered as one of the playing staff with the FA in August of that year.

Doyle's natural love for wheeling and dealing never left him and, whilst back home in Scotland during the close season, the activities of this future Celtic captain, superstar and idol of the fans, almost led to those who came to hero-worship Doyle losing their favourite player of the day, Willie Groves. The Everton registration document of the summer of 1889, now in the archives of The National Football Museum at Preston, shows both Doyle and Groves as having been registered on 15 August. On Willie Groves' Everton player's contract, now lost, it was noted, by the *Glasgow Observer*'s 'Man in the Know' on 1 August 1914, that the witness was Daniel Doyle of Rawyards and that Dan, he suggested, had played a bigger part in the luring away of Groves – another old Hibs teammate – than merely witnessing the document. Fortunately for the Celts, Willie had a quick change of heart and, with the help of Tom Maley, things were quickly sorted out although Everton threatened to sue Groves. But it was just that, a threat.

Dan's initial attempt at being an agent hadn't succeeded and, in his philosophical attitude to setbacks, the irrepressible Dan no doubt smiled and got on with his life. The Celtic supporters were not so forgiving. He was a natural favourite with the Irish not only because he was the son of an Irish father but also because of his previous connection with Hibs. But, when he appeared in the Everton side which played Celtic at Parkhead in October 1889, Doyle was given a pretty hot reception. It was no doubt wryly received by the bold boy who had a tendency to smile his way through adversity and he would have shrugged it off as being nobody's business but his own since, all through his life, he maintained and vigorously exercised the right to please himself in whatever he did. Doyle bowed to no one, rightly or wrongly, such was his faith in his own ability and assessment of his own worth.

His move to Everton was a shrewd one for there they honed his talents into those of the best left back in Britain and his partnership with fellow-Scot Andrew Hannah became legendary. Doyle repaid them handsomely and the man who was destined to remain one of the greatest left backs in Britain for almost a decade helped Everton to second place in the League Championship in season 1889/90 and to the Championship itself in season 1890/91. His popularity, skill and leadership qualities were such that he was voted team captain for the coming season – though it was to be a season he'd spend not in Liverpool with Everton but with Celtic in Glasgow's East End.

Whatever shenanigans Doyle got up to off the field and despite his fast and loose dealings with committeemen and directors, his uncompromising style and commitment to winning raised him to heights of adulation in the eyes of the large Irish population in

Liverpool who followed the Toffeemen. Whenever Doyle played for Celtic or Scotland in that great city in the years to come, he was always given an outstanding reception by fans who hadn't wanted to lose him. But lose him they did under the most bitter of circumstances.

Doyle was once described as having a mind like a weathervane – liable to go off in multiple directions at any time. Fortunately for Glasgow's Irish, when it came to rest in August 1891, it pointed in the direction of Celtic Park.

2

No Holds Barred

Born in Paisley in September 1864, Doyle had been raised in Rawyards near Airdrie since he was six years old, having gone there shortly after the death of his father. His mother and siblings always remained in Paisley where his mother remarried in 1872. The family circle he grew up in consisted mainly of Felix and John Doyle, his uncle and cousin, both of whom were employed in the mining industry, and the matriarch of the family, his aunt Cecilia Doyle. The living conditions in the Rawyards that Doyle knew as a child were described in an article in the *Glasgow Herald* of 1875 by Alexander McDonald, a former Lanarkshire coalminer who, before he entered parliament as a Liberal MP, had been the foremost leader of the British miners and, for a time, the whole of the trade union movement. McDonald was investigating the living conditions of miners in the Clyde Valley and described Rawyards as having 'ashpits and closets filthy in the extreme and the road in front of the houses as no more than a dirty puddle'. That Doyle had an abiding love for it all his life says much for the community who lived there and the ability of the spirit of the miners and their families to rise above the hardships they endured.

The restless and ambitious Doyle had relatives who were constantly on the move between the coalfields of Scotland and it probably surprised no one when he took to the road himself around 1885 and, when working in the mining area around Falkirk, was persuaded to turn out for one of the local teams, Slamannan Barnsmuir. According to Doyle himself, the invitation to play centre forward in a local cup tie against Grahamstown, came from a man whose own character was bound to be admired by the ever-outspoken, though when necessary eloquent, Dan, namely R. Chisholm Robertson, the local miners' agent.

Chisholm Robertson has since been described as a stormy petrel in the mining politics of the late nineteenth and early twentieth centuries and no doubt he had much in common with the potential loose cannon that was Doyle. A friend of J. Keir Hardie, Chisholm Robertson ran the gamut of official positions in national mining union politics and the Glasgow Trades Council before falling foul of the more pragmatic elements because of his lack of moderation when it came to workers' rights and strike tactics. This Scargill-type figure would probably have achieved iconic status during the 1984–85 miners' strike. His ability as an orator, his stubbornness and his outspokenness mirrored Doyle's to a great extent but Dan could temper all of the fieriness with diplomacy when it was required to achieve his own goal. The end always justified the means for Doyle and, unlike Robertson, self-sacrifice was never on the agenda.

Chisholm Robertson was also a member of the Irish National League as were some of the Celtic committee and he often called on the club's support in the form of charity matches in the face of colliery disasters and lock-outs. Perhaps, by encouraging Doyle to set his sights higher, this renegade of the Miners' Union had inadvertently set in motion an inevitable collision between the new Irish team and the fledgling footballer who was Allan Doyle of County Down's first-born son. Either way, Doyle was eventually to follow Robertson's example when, in 1898, along with James Miller of Rangers, he was the driving force behind the new Players' Union in Scotland and its first chairman.

After Slamannan Barnsmuir, Doyle's game was nurtured in the highly charged atmosphere of, firstly, Broxburn Shamrock and, then, East Stirlingshire, both teams noted for their do-or-die style of playing. The Shamrock was one of several teams in the Lothians mining area and yet another Irish Catholic one and it was with them that he began to learn his footballing trade. And, in their rough-and-tumble style, he learned it well, forsaking the centre forward position for that of left back, a position he'd eventually play in for Scotland.

Doyle played for the Shamrock around 1886 and the *Scottish Umpire* noted that there was an entry in the minutes of the Edinburgh Association for 21 December 1886 which is very enlightening when one reflects on a later event in Doyle's somewhat turbulent career and especially in his fraught dealings with a certain English referee.

The Edinburgh Association had received a letter from Broxburn Shamrock. In the letter, Broxburn Shamrock stated that they wanted to appeal the decision of the Edinburgh Association to debar three of their players and the Broxburn Shamrock official who had acted as umpire (today he'd be called an assistant referee) at a previous game against Hearts. The behaviour of all four men had been deemed reprehensible and they'd been banned from taking part in any further competitions arranged under the auspices of the Edinburgh Association that season. Here is what the minutes say about the matter:

> A letter was read from the Broxburn Shamrock desiring that their case should be reconsidered. It will be remembered that three of their players and their umpire were disqualified for grossly insulting the referee, Mr Smith jnr of HMFC [Heart of Midlothian FC]. They petitioned the Association that their case should be reopened and offered to bring the whole eleven players to Edinburgh as they believed there had been a miscarriage of justice. They also broadly hinted that the referee had selected the good players rather than the good swearers. The Committee, however, refused their prayer and, considering the nature of the offence and bearing in mind that the penalty administered to the Champfleurie had been ineffectual in deterring the Shamrock from offending, debarred these players from competing for any Edinburgh Association trophy this season during the pleasure of the Committee.

Doyle was also turning out for East Stirlingshire and Hibernian in the season 1886/87 and whether Doyle was one of the players involved in that game is not known but, in later years, he certainly proved to be equally gifted at both playing and swearing. It was hardly surprising that, being in amongst all of this at the outset, Doyle would find it hard to toe the line with officialdom during the rest of his career.

A week previous to this, the local newspaper also noted that, during an East Stirlingshire v Falkirk match, 'local excitement ran high and at times the language of the onlookers was not of the choicest. When such clubs meet, rough play generally holds sway.' A young footballer had to be tough to survive amongst the teams with whom Doyle spent most of his formative years. There were hard lessons to be learned and learn them he most certainly did.

The years from 1886 to 1888 were something of a disaster for the Shamrock. A miners' strike in the area meant the club, which had recently lost some of its best players to the bigger clubs such as Hibernian, continued to lose players, some looking for work elsewhere and others simply going off to take their chances with the more important teams in Scotland and England. Doyle himself had been recommended to Hibernian by the Shamrock and he began to be seen more frequently in the colours of both Hibernian and East Stirlingshire. Doyle played more for the latter in an amateur era where a man could play for whichever team he wished. He could also play whenever he wanted to, unless he was cup tied for the Scottish Cup.

East Stirlingshire's uncompromising style probably suited him better as Hibernian were a more sedate lot and anyone playing for them had not only to be an Irish Catholic but also a practising one – Dan evidently filling the bill. Broxburn Shamrock suffered greatly from losing its best players at this time but aficionados can look back with pride on the fact that some of the greatest players who ever wore the Celtic colours, such as Barney Battles, Peter Dowds, Alec Brady, Peter Meehan and the greatest Celt of his generation, Dan Doyle, had all first played for the Shamrock.

The illustrious career of the greatest of all Irish teams in Scotland had begun on the bright and pleasant Tuesday evening of 8 May 1888, when Dr Conway, first Honorary President, and Mr Shaughnessy, a committeeman of the Celtic FC, walked on to the field of Celtic Park in Dalmarnock Street, Parkhead, followed by Hibernian and Cowlairs, the teams chosen to hansel the ground. The procession of players was led by James McLaren of Hibernian. The good doctor centred the ball as the five thousand spectators cheered, no doubt immensely proud of the ground they'd virtually built themselves. Men who were quite possibly reluctant to do a hand's turn in the house after a hard day's grind had been more than willing to humph cartloads of earth to get their new Irish team up and not only running but, hopefully, winning.

In those days, women were keen spectators too. They were strong both in body and in mind and it would be interesting to know if they had any part in

15

establishing the ground itself. Under the social and economic conditions prevailing at that time, women often worked longer hours than the men despite the fact that their childbearing was relentless. However, they were advised in the *Scottish Sport* of 3 April 1896 not to go to the international game against England at Celtic Park as there was bound to be squeezing and it was noted that women didn't like that sort of thing. It was a touching sentiment that was bound to have raised a wry smile among the stoical women of Glasgow's East End.

On the pitch that May evening, taking his place at left back for Hibernian, was one Daniel Doyle. Although great things were predicted for him, the comparatively inexperienced Doyle had only just broken into the team. He'd just missed out on a place in the Scottish Cup final of February 1887 in the Hibernian team that beat Dumbarton. Four weeks later the *Airdrie and Coatbridge Advertiser* of 19 March informed the public that local boy Doyle would play at left back for Hibernian against Airdieonians at Mavisbank in aid of the Airdrie miners, the profits being used to pay off the miners' debts for provisions incurred during the recent strike.

While at Hibernian, in May 1888, Doyle played in the Roseberry Cup game against Mossend Swifts at Tynecastle and Hibernian won by a single goal. The team that day contained some names which would be very well known to the West of Scotland Irishmen before Celtic was formed. The team was Felix Docherty, Dan Doyle, Mick McKeown, Paddy Gallacher, Peter McGinn, James McLaren, Paddy

Naughton, James McGhee, Willie Groves, John Coleman and Mick Dunbar.

The day that Hibernian won the Scottish Cup in 1887 in Glasgow was a momentous one in the history of Celtic as it was at a dinner given by the Glasgow Irish supporters to celebrate that victory that the Hibernian secretary, John McFadden, scored a monumental 'own goal' by suggesting that Glasgow should establish its own Irish team and the writing was now on the wall for Hibernian.

Brother Walfrid, the Brother Superior of the Marist teaching order in Glasgow, was present at these celebrations and he took up the suggestion. Eventually, Hibernian would lose seven of its best players to the new club when it was formed on 6 November 1887. Doyle was not one of them for he'd decided to try his luck in the more lucrative market in England. Dan Doyle would forever remain a huge hero with the Irish of the east coast and the Hibernian fans expressed great sorrow and sympathy for him when word of the Cropper tragedy reached them. But amateurism ruled in those days in Scotland and the ambitions Doyle harboured led him to forsake the hand-to-mouth existence of the amateur for it held no attraction for this upwardly mobile miner. It was inevitable that he would tread the path that had been well worn by the Scottish players before him who were, at that time, the backbone of English football.

Doyle would spend the summer of 1888 in the south with Sunderland and was unavailable for the friendly Hibernian v Celtic game on 4 August. He had returned by the end of that month but, when

Hibernian crashed out of the Scottish Cup despite his assistance, Dan headed south once more and, according to Willie Maley in *The Weekly News* of 13 June 1936, he briefly helped out Newcastle East End before making his way to Grimsby, having been head-hunted by their right back, Jimmy Lundie, his old mate from Hibernian.

By this time, the Football League had been formed. It was the brainchild of a Perthshire Scot, William McGregor of Aston Villa, who had insisted on the title 'Football League' rather than 'English League' in the hope that Scottish teams might one day take part and it was to a League club that Doyle was now determined to go. The ambitious Doyle, with one or both eyes on the main chance, selected Everton from several clubs, such as Sunderland and Bolton Wanderers, who wanted him and he headed for Liverpool with, no doubt, a hard-thrashed-out contract in his pocket for Doyle was an astute negotiator and loved the intrigue, the cut and thrust of the chase, almost as much as the end result.

He was also a born gambler but his excessive demands and the threats he employed during his career, whenever renegotiating his contract, were really no gamble to him at all for he knew he stood to lose nothing if his brinkmanship didn't come off as his talents were always in demand elsewhere. Talent he had in abundance and this was coupled, in his Celtic team-mate Tom Maley's words, 'with brain' which he used to great effect, especially on the big occasion.

Doyle loved grandstanding and the 'grandstandites' loved Doyle. He played in all of Everton's twenty-two league matches in 1889/90 and helped the club to the runners-up place in the Championship. He was again registered for Everton the following season and was present in twenty of the twenty-two games played. becoming part of an Everton team that was judged to be one of the greatest that club had ever had – Smalley, Hannah and Doyle; Kirkwood, Holt and Parry; Latta, Brady, Geary, Chadwick and Milward. Hannah and Doyle, both Scots, were reckoned to be 'giant barriers, tacklers and sensational kickers' and the best pairing in English football. Some of the best English players of the day were in this side and five of the team were Scots.

Brady and Doyle, fellow lodgers in Coniston Street, Liverpool, eventually joined Celtic in 1891, taking advantage of the SFA's temporary amnesty which allowed professional players returning to Scotland to be reinstated as amateurs. On their Everton registration form for the season 1891/92 in The National Football Museum in Preston, the word 'whitewashed' is written against both names as Everton no longer expected them to play for the club although they were still officially Everton players in England. The 1890/91 season brought the realisation of Everton's wildest dreams when the team won the FA League Championship having been runners-up to Preston North End the previous season.

Everton had begun the season in style, with sixteen goals being notched up in only four games. The team then came north of the Border in October to play a friendly against Third Lanark, the kick-off being at 12.30 p.m. as Celtic were playing Sunderland in another friendly at 4 p.m. at Parkhead and this allowed the fans to take in both games if they wished.

The Scottish members of the Everton team had left Liverpool two days before the rest of the team in order to spend some time with their families. This would have given Doyle plenty of time to look up his old mates now playing with Celtic and no doubt he was the object of the persuasive utterings of John Glass whose silver tongue was famous or infamous, depending on where one's allegiance lay. Doyle was never an unwilling participant in these nefarious activities. The game against Thirds ended in a draw and it's not recorded whether or not the Everton players, after their tram ride back into the city, went to watch the game at Parkhead.

Later that season, Everton played their last league game of the season and lost away from home to Burnley which meant they were now pinning their hopes of a League Championship victory on the great Preston North End losing to Sunderland that same day. This they duly did, losing 3–0 away from home, and Doyle and the rest of the team were now the recipients of a £5 bonus and a gold medal from a grateful Everton.

Unfortunately for Everton, they eventually discovered that a contract with the congenial Dan wasn't worth the paper it was written on when the 'bould bhoy's' hyperactive mind decided once more he'd had enough – or not quite enough. Doyle smiled his way through everything all his life and what left committeemen and directors outraged merely raised yet another smile on the handsome face – the implication being that they should have known better.

Doyle always returned home to Airdrie whenever he had the chance and, despite the immense self-confidence and the ability to savour all aspects of life wherever he went, his love for the company and pursuits of the Lanarkshire mining community forever held him in its thrall. In April 1891, his mother died in Paisley and Doyle no doubt took this opportunity once back in Scotland to look up his old mates at Parkhead and naturally the Celtic men had a go at 'tapping him up' once again. To their credit, they, by their own admission, had been after him for a long time and were not about to give up. There can be no doubt that Celtic were desperate to have him for he'd already promised to sign for the 'amateurs' the previous summer. Doyle, being generous to a fault with his promises, had said the same thing to J. J. Bentley of Bolton Wanderers and had taken close season's wages from both that team and Everton – and possibly Celtic too.

Doyle was right, Everton should have read the signs when it came to relying on his word, both oral and written, and the debacle which followed in the summer of 1891 could have been avoided. They should have realised that a contract signed on 1 May 1891, keeping him at Everton until 30 April 1893 with £100 paid up front as an advance on his wages for season 1891/92, was no barrier to Dan Doyle when he decided to renegotiate his contract or move to Celtic. And 'amateur' Celtic were more than willing to accommodate him in every way such was their desire to get Doyle on their books.

Doyle had got wind that the £3 a week he was being paid was less than some of his team-mates were getting and, to Doyle, that meant it was open season on Everton. The fact that Everton trusted the quixotic Dan so much must surely stem from previous dealings with him. These had led to the labels 'Daniel, the Man of Principle' and 'Daniel the Incorruptible' being applied by the Everton officials to him and must, in some way, explain the trust they placed in their left back's word.

Doyle's desire to extract more reward for his labours than he'd previously wrought from Everton coincided with the SFA's amnesty for all returning players who wished to be reinstated as amateurs. When the opportunity arose, Doyle frequently returned home to Airdrie to take part in quoiting matches and the like. During these visits, he had probably seen the developing situation in Scotland and would have viewed it as an ideal opportunity to flex his muscles in the football market of the day.

The Everton supporters must have been alarmed when Doyle's name began to appear in the English papers coupled with that of the 'amateur' club, Celtic. One newspaper, the *Athletic News,* stated that the very idea that Doyle would want to cross the Border, having been paid good maintenance money for the summer, to join Celtic purely for the love of the game was remarkable. A fair proportion of the Everton Championship-winning side were Scots and, of them, they had already lost Andrew Hannah, Doyle's partner at the back and the team captain, to Renton in May of the same year and Alec Brady was also threatening to move north to Celtic. Even the *Scottish Sport* wondered at players like Doyle, Brady and McCallum of Nottingham Forrest leaving English teams to come to Celtic to live on 'fresh air' though, of course, this was pure sarcasm. But to say Doyle was definitely signing for Celtic was undoubtedly premature.

Along with Alec Brady, Dan Doyle applied for reinstatement as an amateur at the end of July. At the same time, they were joined in this by Neil McCallum, the man who, in May 1888, had scored the first-ever goal for the new club, Celtic.

At the Celtic Sports, held at the beginning of August 1891, a rumour circulated that two unnamed Everton players would turn out for the Celts and, by doing so, they'd be committing themselves to the club for the season. Both Doyle and Brady were in the pavilion but, no matter how much cajoling and coaxing was done, neither one would strip and play either then or subsequently at Greenock or Airdrie.

Doyle was still hedging his bets. When, in July, Everton had first got wind of their star player's intention, they lost no time in confronting the unfaithful Dan. *Field Sports* recorded in August that the Everton committeemen had said that they'd 'see Doyle ****** hang first' before they would let him go. Eventually Doyle informed them by letter in late July that he'd applied to be reinstated as an amateur in Scotland and intended playing for Celtic. Everton's response to this letter was to send a deputation to Doyle's Scottish home to persuade him to return. This he refused to do unless they could match Celtic's terms. When reminded that he'd already signed for Everton for the next two years at £3 a week, two thirds of which had been paid to him on signing, Doyle simply stated that he'd been given advice that the agreement couldn't be legally enforced.

When asked what Celtic's offer was, Doyle had no hesitation in saying that it was the tenancy of a public house, which would yield him £5 a week, plus payment for each match he played in. If this were so, the foolhardy and loquacious Dan had dropped Celtic right in it as, in 1891, Scottish football was still strictly amateur. When asked what he wanted of Everton, Doyle graciously consented to return to the club if the committee would give him £100 for the previous two years and increase the present wage agreement from £3 to £4 per week.

The committeemen were horrified at such an exorbitant demand and one wonders if Doyle was ever in fact seriously thinking of returning south at all. Money, generally speaking, was the prime motive for Doyle but he was also a willing participant in mind games. He enjoyed wielding power over directors and committeemen. Employers had made plenty of money from the likes of miners such as Doyle and, for his part, Doyle was into role reversal in a big way. Already a hardened coal-miner by the age of sixteen, Doyle had learned a lot during those dark days down the pit and he knew exactly how to get his pound of flesh. There was never any animosity on his part in his dealings, just a steely determination to get his own way, and, in this case, the gambler in Doyle knew he held the winning hand. Whichever way it went, he simply couldn't lose.

When Doyle appeared before a four-man committee in Liverpool on 1 August, he was informed that, if they agreed to his terms, the other players would be entitled to be placed on the same footing and the club's finances couldn't withstand that. He was, however, offered a slight increase since he'd been voted captain for the coming season. Doyle magnanimously accepted this offer and said that he was returning home to take part in a quoiting match.

Quoiting was a popular miners' pastime that involved throwing heavy iron discs at posts embedded in concrete a fair distance away. Requiring great stamina and skill, it was a game Doyle loved and, of course, he expected to win whenever he played – not least because big money changed hands in these games. It also had an added bonus – the amount of practice Doyle put in plus the training he'd promised the Everton committee he'd undertake whilst in Scotland would ensure he was extremely fit by the time the beginning of the new football season came round.

He gave the committee great assurances of his satisfaction with the deal that had been done and pledged his fidelity to the club. He was presumably satisfied with the result of the meeting and, on the afternoon of the same day that he was interviewed by the Everton officials in Liverpool, he fired off telegrams to various newspapers saying that he was definitely returning to Everton. The *Athletic News* reported that it had received one from him showing, it said, the latest whim of the Everton back – 'Kindly insert I intend playing for Everton, certain.' It also remarked that, after the way he'd enjoyed himself during the previous three years at various English clubs, no one could be blamed for not relying on his word. If it were so obvious that Doyle was indeed not a man of his word, why had Everton trusted him at all?

A week later, on Saturday 8 August, he wired Everton to say that he intended playing for Celtic on the Monday against Cowlairs and this he duly did. So despite the negotiations and his assurances that he was happy and would definitely be back at Everton, Doyle was now a Celtic player. Brady also signed for the club.

It was hinted in the English papers that Celtic and the other Scottish clubs would be the losers as it was possible that a general retribution would be exacted with the English clubs refusing to play Scottish teams who intended fielding players whose registrations were still held by the FA. That was not the financial hardship it would once have been for, since the formation of the Scottish League in 1890, most teams were by now too taken up with league games and cup ties to play lucrative friendlies against English teams as often as they had in the past. The only team unaffected would be Queen's Park as it had no 'whitewashed' players – 'all are pure, undefiled amateurs' (*Scottish Sport*, 15 September 1891).

Everton did not take this lying down and reported to the FA that Celtic had offered better terms to Doyle than they had. 'Suspicious' was the word used to describe the goings-on between 'amateur' Celtic and the worldly-wise Doyle. The chances, however, of proving that Celtic would be the provider of the public house were negligible since the club's other player/publicans had had the capital provided for them by ardent Celtic supporters and not the club itself. It was, no doubt, a convenient arrangement but *Scottish Sport* rightly noted that, although this distinction was small, it would be enough to prevent the SFA from interfering. Why Doyle had actually let slip the details of his secret negotiations with the Celts is not so much down to it being a mystery as to Dan having opened his mouth and put his foot in it. The saving grace for Celtic, as Everton were to realise in the end, was that Doyle had gone 'round the houses' so much that nobody could rely on anything he said and, consequently, all the tales he'd told them concerning his proposed dealings with Celtic didn't amount to much. When Everton said he'd lied to them before, how could anyone now be expected to believe that his version of his conversations with the Celtic officials was true? Everton should have read the *Athletic News* a bit more carefully.

There was a certain sympathy in the Scottish press for the predicament Everton found themselves in but the Scottish clubs had been the victims of the unrelenting poaching of their finest players for years and the turning of the tables was met with a great degree of satisfaction in Scotland in general. Everton could always attempt to get financial revenge in the law courts. The downside was that, if it could be proved that 'amateur' Celtic were actually infringing the rules by paying Doyle, the club would be banned in Scotland by the SFA and, as a result of the proposed ban by English teams on playing against 'whitewashed' players of whom Celtic had more than a few, the weakened team would not be attractive opposition to English sides. The only source of revenue then left open to Celtic would have gone. Celtic stood a fair chance of going to the wall.

Dan Doyle was indeed a loose cannon and why the hard-headed Celtic committeemen had not made contingency plans for this is the real mystery. Doyle, of course, was not in this alone but Brady eventually managed to settle his differences with Everton and paid back the £36 he owed them. If Doyle had wanted to, he could have claimed he'd been grossly libelled by Everton as it was only their word against his. There was no written evidence at all.

By now, Doyle was keeping uncharacteristically quiet. If the matter did come before the SFA, it was assumed he would only admit to the public house part but insist that it was to be a gift from his Celtic-supporting fairy godfather. The *Scottish Sport* wrote that 'the Association has no jurisdiction over individual members of the Celtic, it cannot touch those open-handed donors who gift away public houses to players of note who require that inducement to play for the Irish combination'.

On 14 September, the Football Association wrote to the SFA setting out Everton's case in a rather half-hearted manner. Eventually the SFA were given copies of registration forms but the FA asked the Scots to investigate only 'if they saw fit' as it appeared one of their clubs was breaking their rules. The SFA wrote back asking if they were being requested to investigate the Celtic actions, pointing out they would do so 'only as an act of courtesy' towards the FA. The reply was that the FA had no wish or desire in the matter and, although the Celtic representatives plus Doyle and Brady were on hand to give evidence at an SFA meeting, they were not required to do so and the matter was dropped. So

Doyle was not only whitewashed, he was officially as pure as the driven snow.

The Everton men were on a hiding to nothing as they were pilloried in the English press for allowing two of their best players to leave over the matter of a few pounds. Everton's only recourse now was to commence legal proceedings against Doyle for breach of agreement and the return of the money given him as wages he hadn't earned, a case which would be eagerly awaited in the Glasgow law courts.

Dan Doyle placed his case in the hands of Mr Joseph Shaughnessy, a Celtic official, and the club must have prayed the loose cannon they'd tried so hard to acquire wouldn't blow up in their faces. On 10 January 1892, the case of 'Mr R Molyneux on behalf of Everton FC against Daniel Doyle, lately residing at 26 Coniston St, Liverpool and now residing at Marlborough St, Glasgow' came before the Glasgow Sheriff Court. Everton maintained they'd paid Doyle £100 as part of the agreement between club and player on 1 May 1891 and, in violation of contract, he'd deserted Everton and was induced to join the Celtic FC.

Doyle admitted receiving the money and terminating the contract on 8 August 1891 but maintained he'd only joined Celtic because it was closer to his home in Airdrie. (Obviously the notion of a public house had been thrust upon him at a later date!) He also stated that he'd served Everton for fourteen weeks (the time since 1 May which included the close season). He said his wages for this period amounted to £42 and that he was, and always had been, willing to return the balance to the club on their discharging

29

their claims against him. The case was due to be debated at a later date.

On 4 March, it was recorded that the case had been settled amicably out of court. On 24 May, *Scottish Sport* reported that 'amongst sums noted on the Everton balance sheet as being due the club is £69 from Doyle. It was paid last Saturday.' Doyle had obviously managed to hold on to the other £31!

After all this trouble, it is remarkable to note what lengths Everton then went to in trying to persuade Doyle to leave Celtic and rejoin Everton in 1894. Both Celtic and Everton obviously thought that the performances Dan put in on the pitch were well worth all the grief he regularly gave them.

3

The Return of the Prodigal

The summer of 1891 saw Celtic not only having to deal with the quicksilver mind of Doyle and the mounting anger of Everton, whose officials had always been on excellent terms with the Celtic committeemen, but also the equally inexplicable behaviour of their landlord. *Scottish Sport* reported that the Celtic landlord had fixed the terms of renewing the lease of the ground at such a high figure that he was practically forcing the club out and questioned if, in fact, this was the real motive behind it. They suggested that 'the wily landlord stands a good chance of having the ground left on his hands'. The newspaper also suggested that clubs should consider buying their grounds and thus give themselves not only security but also a good investment – advice which Celtic finally took in 1897.

If the summer of 1892 had left Dan Doyle £69 poorer and a pub richer, it also saw him the proud owner of a Scottish Cup-winner's medal. Doyle will always be remembered as a vital member of the Three

Cup Team season 1891/92 when Celtic, Glasgow's 'Irish' team, finally came good. This came after the supporters' hopes had been raised in their first-ever season when Celtic were the beaten finalists in 1889's 'snow final'. This had been a massive boost to Irish morale then and it left the club and supporters with the knowledge that soon, very soon, with the right men, they would finally make it to the top in Scottish football.

The Scottish Cup was what it was all about in those days as the League was in its infancy, having only been formed in 1890. This team of 1891/92 came together partly as a result of the SFA's temporary amnesty for returning professionals who wished to be reinstated as amateur. Amongst the more ordinary players returning from England who formed the bulk of the hundred or more Anglos were a dozen or so gems of whom Celtic took – or enticed – more than a few of the best to grace Celtic Park. This team and season have gone down in the history of the club as one of the greatest, with the team winning the Scottish Cup, the Glasgow Cup and the Glasgow Charity Cup as well as coming second in the League Championship to Dumbarton, a team which played only half the number of competitive games throughout the season that Celtic had.

Doyle played for Celtic on 10 August 1891 against Cowlairs and, thereby, committed himself to the club – much to the delight of the Celtic supporters and the chagrin of Everton. Celtic was the club he would remain with for the rest of his career despite the annual resigning merry-go-round that was designed to let committeemen know who was boss and for everyone else to understand that his services could never be taken for granted. There was no doubting that the committeemen were delighted to have finally landed the man who, as an Irish Catholic from the West of Scotland, was already regarded by them and the supporters as theirs by right anyway.

Scottish Sport's 'A Puffer' lets us see in his report how the Celtic 'high heid yins' reacted to Doyle turning out that eventful evening and how closely it mirrored that of the ordinary bhoy on the terracing.

> I can't remember when I saw so much jubilation among the Celtic officials as was evidenced on Monday night. On entering the Cowlairs' enclosure, Mr O'Hara button-holed me and there was a mischievous twinkle in his eye as he quietly whispered – 'I'm sorry you're too late for the names of the teams but perhaps you can distinguish the men for yourself.' There was something in his manner I did not quite understand but glancing over his shoulder in the direction of the players, I was astonished to see the Everton cracks, Doyle and Brady. I felt inclined to shout 'hurroo!' and in the excitement, I almost extinguished the light of day from Mr McLaughlin's left optic with a lighted 'Caporal'. The latter tried hard not to grin but there was an itching around the corners of his mouth which betrayed his ill-concealed attempts to puff on complacently. Mr Curtis wrung my hand. He was too full of emotion to give utterance to the great joy he was experiencing. The Celtic have triumphed in this matter and Scotchmen are delighted that English clubs are being left in the lurch – that some measure of retribution is being meted out to them. Bravo Celts!

Celtic at last had Doyle and, with Jerry Reynolds partnering him at the back, they were now deemed supreme in defence, Tom Duff being the new goal-keeper. Unfortunately, as time went by, Duff suffered badly from rheumatism and, after the disastrous Ne'erday friendly game against Dumbarton at the back end of the winter when Celtic were beaten 8–0, he retired and was replaced by the great Joe Cullen. Willie Maley blamed that defeat on the time of year and the joke going the rounds was that it was the result of Celtic fielding a team who 'ate' nothing. Liquid celebrations and football very evidently did not mix.

On 15 September 1891, this team was described in *Scottish Sport* as potentially a great one – 'grandly balanced throughout, gifted with energy, requisite of skill, speed and physical development to cope with the most powerful eleven in Scotland'. 'Bring on the Cups!' was the battle cry and that's what duly happened. In the debut against Cowlairs, the supporters having already seen Doyle in both the Hibs and Everton jerseys, now saw him in the green and white vertical stripes of Celtic for the first time. His kicking and accurate tackling received loud praise and no one seemed particularly upset when the Bhoys went in 3–1 down at half-time.

Although it took Doyle some time to settle in, his game improved as the match progressed. A final score of 6–3 for Celtic left the Doyle debut unblemished and all were satisfied that Celtic had found a true successor to the brilliant but woefully wayward Mick McKeown. Eventually it was written of this great team that 'there is a bond existing between the players which is hard to sever and which is the keynote to success' ('Granuaile', *Scottish Football Association*

Annual, 1892–93). These men were great friends for many years both on and off the field and this was probably a factor in keeping Doyle at Celtic Park – as well as the financial consideration, of course.

Apparently Celtic's president, John Glass, had arrived at Cowlairs' ground in a cab before the game, closely guarding Doyle and Brady as, in those amateur days, clubs could lose players at any moment. Nobody knew better than Celtic how fraught the business of keeping a player safe until he'd officially turned out for the club was – they were themselves past masters at 'kidnapping' players both in Scotland and in England.

In September, Celtic met Abercorn at Paisley and Doyle's appearance, 'that of a star of the first magnitude' (*Scottish Sport*, 15 September 1891), plus the excellent weather drew a crowd of seven thousand, a large proportion coming from Glasgow's East End to support the Bhoys who'd now embarked on a decent run of victories. There was never any doubt of Celtic's superiority but Abercorn put their best eleven on the field to face them and were determined to put up as hard a struggle as possible but, by half-time, Celtic were leading 3–2. The Bhoys turned on the style in the second half, their famous dodging and intricate passing helping them to a final score in their favour of 5–2. *Scottish Sport* noted that:

> when the Celts stepped onto the field, there was no mistaking the sympathy of the majority of the large crowd. The special trains, groaning under the living freight, had come from Parkhead, while every good Irishman in Paisley and district went out to cheer the 'bould bhoys'.

Quite a few would probably have been related to Doyle as his mother and siblings had lived there until she had died there earlier in the year. His mother's family had lived in Paisley for over thirty years although his maternal grandparents had been born in Ireland. It was also noted that, although it was Doyle's name that was on everybody's lips, he didn't play as well as Jerry Reynolds that day. Doyle's name would have been on everybody's lips except for those of the Reynolds' fans who stampeded towards Jerry at Gilmour Street station in 'a remarkable display of hero worship' (*Scottish Sport*, 15 September 1891).

All the while, Doyle was still embroiled in his battle with Everton. It was reported that the majority of the Celtic players had appeared wearing thin silk pants and that during the game, at least four of them had to resort to wearing trews 'to cover their nakedness. These luxuries may feed the vanity of vain men but, for a hard football contest, they don't quite suit' was the opinion of *Scottish Sport* on 15 September 1891. This league game against Abercorn was the first to see the new penalty-kick rule demonstrated and it went against the home team. But, when Andrew Duff saved Johnny Madden's attempt, there was a tremendous cheer. When first introduced, the kick could be taken then from any point along a twelve-yard line.

The pre-season friendlies had got Celtic off to a great start that season and, by winning all three, their confidence was sky-high. Doyle was still not rated as good as McKeown by his critics in the press but merely 'safe when there's a rush on' (*Scottish Sport*, 25 August 1891). The opening league game saw Celtic away to Hearts and they came down to earth with a bang, being soundly beaten 3–1. Fortunately the hard lessons learned in that game stood them in good stead for the rest of the season and Doyle very soon proved what a class back he was.

The team were now more than ready for their first encounter of the new season with Rangers at home. It was unfortunate for Rangers that they met when Celtic were still smarting from that humiliation at Tynecastle. They had indeed been comprehensively thrashed and were out to delete it from the memory bank. That day, the team played like fury in front of some twelve thousand spectators. A scoreless first half gave way to a right battle royal, 'more vigorous than scientific' (*Scottish Sport*, 25 August 1891), and remarkable for the speed of play until Sandy McMahon opened the scoring with an amazing screw kick. Campbell and Madden took the hint and added to Celtic's account and the team enjoyed a thoroughly deserved 3–0 victory which restored a little self-respect in their own eyes.

One critic decided that any team coming up against Celtic in that mood would have to fight very hard indeed to gain a victory. This was Doyle's first league game in front of the Celtic faithful at Parkhead and Cullen of the Rangers failed to make any headway against him at all. Celtic now embarked on a series of good victories in the league.

Meanwhile, in September, the Football Association issued an edict banning all reinstated players whose registrations were still held by English clubs from playing matches in England. They only sanctioned their appearances in international games as this was their right by birth and, apparently, only allowing this concession as they knew that no other Association would stand for such an autocratic interference in its business. Celtic were now under a potential cloud as their team included not only Doyle and Brady but also Neil McCallum, who'd returned under the amnesty from Nottingham Forrest, and a Celtic minus these names would prove less attractive opposition.

The Glasgow Cup was the first of the major trophies to be won that season and Celtic played Kelvinside Athletic, Partick Thistle, Northern (including a replay against them) and then Linthouse in the semi-final. The competition's origins lay in an SFA meeting of 10 May 1887 which decreed that all Scottish clubs should withdraw from the FA Cup and cease competing for that trophy. In other words, Scottish clubs were to decide which Association they wished to belong to. This, of course, was Hobson's choice. As no league had yet been formed in Scotland or England either at that time, this left Scottish clubs with only one major trophy to compete for – the Scottish Cup. Friendlies now would be the only other source of revenue apart from anything gained in minor competition. So, in order to offset this financial loss, the Glasgow Cup was introduced in season 1887/88 and it was such a success that, at times in years to come, as many as one hundred thousand spectators attended finals between Celtic and Rangers.

In their bid to retain the trophy they'd won the previous season, Celtic, having disposed of Linthouse in the semi-final, now found Clyde the opposition at Cathkin Park. The weather was atrocious, with heavy rain ceaselessly pummelling those of the faithful six thousand who were exposed to the elements that day. Celtic led 2–0 at half-time but, just after the restart, Clyde gave their supporters hope by pulling one back and this seemed to trigger a change in the weather from rain to snow. Celtic moved up a gear and those spectators still braving the cold at full-time applauded a Celtic team who'd won the Glasgow Cup 7–1, under the most trying of conditions. Several of the Clyde players, the chill proving too much for them, had actually collapsed.

This was Doyle's first medal won with Celtic and a handsome one it was too. Celtic could now boast of having won that Cup twice in the same year as in the previous season the final against Third Lanark had been postponed from December 1890 to February 1891 due to bad weather and congestion of fixtures and the Bhoys had won it 4–0.

The team who beat Clyde was: Duff, Reynolds, Doyle; Dowds, Kelly, Maley; Brady, McCallum, Madden, Campbell and McMahon. At the Visitor Centre at Celtic Park, there is a medal won that day by Peter Dowds and it's on loan to Celtic courtesy of Bill Daly, a Celtic supporter, who has a fascinating story as to how it came into his family's possession. In the words of Willie Maley:

> Dowds was a wonderful footballer. His versatility was unique. Talk about class all-rounders . . . There has never and I don't think ever will be, finer. It did not matter in which position Peter played, he distinguished himself. He was the perfect middle-man. He did not need to throw himself about to get contact. Contact came to him by his own intuition.

Dowds left Celtic for Aston Villa and then Stoke, before returning north to Celtic two years after he left. But Peter was very ill and died young in 1895 of consumption.

The players were obviously not on bonus that vile day they won the Glasgow Cup and when William Daly, Bill's grandfather, met his friend Peter Dowds one day in Paisley and asked him what he'd got for winning, no doubt thinking of a bonus, Dowds brought out the medal from his pocket and said 'That!' He then dropped the much-coveted medal and kicked it as it fell, sending it into some nearby grass, before walking on. Mr Daly went back to the spot the following day and, after much searching, found the little gold object and took it back to the Celtic man. Dowds refused it and told him to keep it. Medals didn't bring a working man money in those pre-eBay days!

Celtic were fortunate in having players, such as forwards Sandy McMahon and Johnny Campbell, who were at the peak of their careers, and those two men were inseparable friends, their understanding of each other's game second to none. The other three forwards, Alec Brady, Johnny Madden and Neil McCallum, epitomised a quiet and very dangerous style of play, Madden in particular being extremely elusive. Behind these five, ranged a fearless, solid defence who were more than capable of dealing with the best the other teams could throw at them. Doyle slotted in brilliantly, providing Celtic's most formidable pairing ever at the back with Jerry Reynolds.

As already mentioned, Ne'erday 1892 brought Celtic's mean machine to an abrupt halt in that game against Dumbarton which, fortunately, was only a friendly. Celtic's only consolation was the fact that Dumbarton were, in turn, beaten 7–1 by Hearts the following day. These were the days when the New Year was the most important day to be celebrated in a big way – with the national drink, of course – as Christmas was not regarded like it is today although, over a hundred years later, we seem to be reverting to type once more. Consequently, the Celtic players were being truly patriotic.

This game saw the end of Tom Duff's career and the junior club Benburb's Joe Cullen was pitchforked into the team. Doyle's game was in no way affected by his imminent lawsuit with Everton concerning his broken contract – the Ne'erday game notwithstanding – and he had a great game against Rangers at the beginning of January, his kicking apparently quite brilliant. Celtic now had their sights firmly on the biggest trophy of them all, the Scottish Cup.

Cullen played for the first time in the game against Cowlairs and was on the winning side, conceding only one goal to his opposite number's four. Celtic had already beaten St Mirren 4–2 at Paisley in front of a crowd of four thousand, also beating Kilmarnock Athletic at Parkhead 3–0, thus setting themselves up for the game with Cowlairs.

Now the semi-final saw them take on Rangers on 6 February at home before a crowd of eleven thousand and, by the interval, they were already four goals up and cruising to victory. If anyone had left to catch a train or a dog cart (a favourite means of transportation in the Lanarkshire villages), they missed a nail-biting second half as Rangers came out fighting – qualities the Celts thought were theirs alone. The Bhoys soon found they had a fight on their hands and their lead was cut to 4–3. Fortunately, Doyle's fellow refugee from Everton, Alec Brady, followed the old Celtic adage that, if you find yourself in front of the goal with no one on your right to pass to and no one on your left to pass to, then just stick the ball in the back of the net and Celtic were now 5–3 up with just minutes to go. Rangers' fate was now sealed and Celtic had made the final with the amateur Queen's Park the opposition, a team with which Celtic had an unofficial agreement never to poach their players.

This was the old regime versus the new and every man, woman and child in Glasgow's East End believed their Bhoys would bring back the coveted Scottish Cup to Parkhead. Celtic's play was based on that of Preston North End – skilful close-passing and dribbling being the order of the day – but the inter-mittent snowfalls of the previous few days had left the ground very slippery by kick-off, which was definitely not conducive to this style of play.

The highly respected Queen's Park had flown the flag for Scottish football for many a long day and, despite their 'play for the sake of playing' ideal, they were not above cutting up rough when the chips were down – as they were to show in the same final the following year. Celtic had come through the hard semi against Rangers and were now eager for the fray, no one more so than Doyle who relished every opportu-nity to show off his footballing ability. On one occasion, he walked from Glasgow's city centre to

Cathkin Park, where a game was to take place, just to get himself toned up for the match. In those days, the Celtic players, as part of their training, were generally dropped off at points some miles from the ground and told to either run or walk back to Celtic Park.

This match was due to take place on 12 March at Ibrox Park and, for this game, Doyle and Reynolds were reckoned to be the equal of Walter Arnott and Robert Smellie, both of whom had already been capped by Scotland against England. All the players were in peak physical condition and a great game was expected, with the entire country reaching fever pitch days before a ball was kicked. The Celtic team were looking forward to playing Queen's Park as they had never beaten them.

The supporters came from all airts and pairts on a cold March day, the usual amount of snow, which was by now almost obligatory at these occasions, having blitzed Glasgow that same week leaving the pitch still frost-bound on the morning of the game. But a quick thaw set in which simply turned a hard surface into a greasy one. The streets around Ibrox Park were thronged with people arriving for the spectacle by every mode of transport possible. The brake clubs, as supporters' clubs were then called, owing to the mode of transport – the brake or charabanc – no doubt added to the colourful, noisy scene with their magnificent banners on that cold, raw day. The pitch was now deemed playable and whether to wear studs or bars was probably the question occupying the Celts' minds as the danger to themselves was probably self-evident.

Doyle's own mind was now free of any impending aggro from Everton as the two parties had settled their differences by this time. Smellie, the Queen's Park left back, was being mooted as such for the forthcoming international against England and the bould Dan was no doubt out to dash that idea once and for all. He had much to prove in this game as he had had a poor performance in the international trials. Doyle was his own worst enemy at times like that as he never condescended to prove himself to anyone and, more often than not, was deliberately a non-trier. Then again, perhaps he was right in thinking players should be judged on club form over a period of time and not on a one-off game.

A lot was riding on this Scottish Cup final, not least of which was Irish pride. Queen's Park were an excellent side and, as they had refused to join the League in 1890, Celtic hadn't had the opportunity to get to know their play intimately. It was, therefore, obviously going to be more difficult to beat the team which, to the Celtic supporters, rightly or wrongly, represented the Establishment.

The excitement was all consuming even before the crowds had entered the ground, with thousands milling around the streets in the area hours before four o'clock, the appointed hour for the kick-off, had been reached. In fact, so great was the crowd that the gates were closed at 2 p.m. and a most impressive if somewhat crushed forty thousand souls were packed like sardines in a tin inside Ibrox Park. The Celtic pony, laden with the players' gear, had managed to keep his hooves in the slush abounding in the southside streets although he did have a tendency to 'take a dive'. In later years, this was believed by the trainer to presage a Celtic defeat and had him weeping openly when it happened.

The pony was one of the lucky ones as he, of course, knew the people who mattered and managed to gain access to the ground – unlike some twenty thousand hopefuls who were locked out. The crowd cheered loudly as the teams came out – so much so that Willie Maley, who'd played the game at all levels, could still hear it ringing in his ears years later as he gave his view of that March day:

> Now Celtic would have won this first game but for the behaviour of the crowd. As the game progressed and the fortunes of the fighters swayed now this way and that, so did the excitement of the crowd rise to a frenzy. We were leading by the only goal scored and were holding Queen's so well that victory looked to be assured. Then came a break-in. I had the ball and was about to throw it in when there was a rush over the touchlines. I was lost in the tide of humanity. The ball was knocked out of my hands and, in trying to recover it, I was almost swept off my feet. I managed to recover my balance and the ball and stood my ground till the crowd was driven back beyond the touchline. But not for long. They came a little later in a greater rush than before and in greater volume, practically enveloping the pitch and making play impossible. Ultimately we managed to play to a finish and retired winners by 1–0. But Queen's Park protested the result on the grounds of crowd behaviour and Celts had to go through it all over again.

This was how Willie Maley recorded it in his life story on Saturday, 13 June 1936 in *The Weekly News*.

There had been one hundred and fifty policemen on duty at this game, some of them mounted. Both sets of officials had actually informed the referee that, because of the conditions of the pitch and crowd disturbances, with prolonged stoppages for order to be restored, they would be protesting and demanding a replay. That Celtic maintained this stance despite winning the game is to their eternal credit. In the first Scottish Cup final Celtic had reached – that of season 1888/89, against Third Lanark – the Thirds had protested against the wintry state of the pitch underfoot in the replay but, having won the game 2–1, they conveniently suffered from amnesia.

The supporters were, as always, the last to know that Celtic had not officially won the Cup after beating Queen's Park – no texting in the good old days! – and many a sore head from celebrating well but not wisely had an additional cause to ache rather badly in the days to come.

Due to the internationals against the Home countries, it was a month before the replay took place, once more at Ibrox. Rangers had given assurances that the improvements, which they'd now carried out, would ensure spectators would be housed more comfortably and, more importantly still, safely. This, therefore, prevented the SFA's original intention of doubling the individual price of entry from one shilling to two from taking place, a measure that would inevitably have victimised the poorer members of society. Nothing changes! This volte-face by the powers that be did not reach the ordinary punter and they very wisely voted with their feet – the Celtic pony's views were probably not canvassed – and, consequently, the crowd at the replay was a mere twenty-two thousand. And so on 9 April, Celtic once more met Queen's Park to do battle for the Scottish Cup.

In the meantime, Doyle had played for Scotland against England and had also been selected for the Scottish League team versus the Football League and much controversy surrounded this game as the FA Council had been informed by John H. McLaughlin of Celtic, the SFA secretary, that, unless they removed the barrier preventing Doyle and Hannah – the famous ex-Everton back division – from playing against English teams, no match would take place. The team would play as selected or not at all. *Scottish Sport* commented, 'Quite right too! A Scotch team without Hannah and Doyle would be like a British fleet at Trafalgar without Nelson and Collingwood!'

The Celtic team was brimming with confidence for the replay although the injured Johnny Madden was missing, with Paddy Gallagher coming into the rearranged side. Queen's Park likewise had to rearrange their side, the legendary Walter Arnott being replaced by Sillars at right back. But Sillars was a great replacement and eventually went on to partner Doyle at the back for Scotland. Celtic's confidence was not misplaced. Willie Maley wrote of this game as being a real eye-opener for Queen's Park's supporters and Celtic lifted the Scottish Cup in style, beating their opponents 5–1 despite losing the first goal of the game.

A Waddell goal meant Celtic went in a goal down at half-time. But that team feared no one and McMahon and Campbell were in a class of their own. That Celtic team brimmed with an unshakeable faith in themselves and it's little wonder that this self-belief soon translated itself into goals. The left-wing pairing of McMahon and Campbell both scored twice. Another was kindly donated to Celtic by the reeling Queen's Parkers and the West of Scotland's Irish population went completely wild. The players in that team were ordinary working-class Irish bhoys and they could easily relate to the ecstatic reactions of the support. A life that was normally pretty grim suddenly became gloriously alive as success of the highest order was bestowed by proxy on every miner, docker, labourer and tradesman. They'd pinned their hopes on the wearers of the green finally coming good in the most spectacular of ways and beaten the nobs at their own game!

As still happens in certain Lanarkshire towns when the Bhoys hit the heights, streets in Glasgow's East End became no-go areas for anyone not interested in wild delight made manifest. My wearing a green-and-white jester's hat with bells on, by way of celebrating the Bhoys' Scottish Cup win in 2004, would have been a massive disappointment to my great-grandfather Daniel Rowan. Originally from Lisnamuck, Maghera, County Derry, he helped celebrate Celtic's massive display of superiority that day in Glasgow in 1892 in great style. And here is how Willie Malley described the events in a series entitled 'Great Celtic Men of the Past' which the *Weekly Record and Mail* ran in 1915 from May to September:

> Our lot stamped themselves that day as champions of Scotland without a doubt and their football was a delight to watch. What a happy lot we were that night when the Cup was taken up to St Mary's Halls by John Glass of happy memory. Poor Glass, he looked as if his chief end in

life had been attained and there was not a happier man in the universe that night. In his speech replying for the club, he reminded his hearers of his prophecy when we were beaten by Third Lanark and told them we would do it yet.

Celtic, once again, had received a massive amount of barracking in that game as the Irish incomers and it rankled eternally. 'Cups won nowadays,' wrote Willie Maley in his book, *The Story of the Celtic*, 'like the Scottish, carry with them bonuses of a substantial size but I may tell those interested that the bonus for the Cup was a suit of clothes for each man.' They'd also been given a £3 bonus. But, before gaining the 'treble', Celtic first had to win the remaining trophy, the Glasgow Charity Cup.

In 1876/77, the merchants of Glasgow had donated a striking trophy, named the Glasgow Charity Cup, to be played for in annual competition on behalf of Glasgow charitable institutions and this cup was the last of the treble Celtic were going for. This competition had the added bonus of being played in early summer and, thus, not only were the players pleased at the prospect of decent weather, the Celtic pony was no doubt even happier when he got the day off as the final was played at Celtic Park that season.

On 1 June, Celtic were scheduled to play Rangers, having already defeated Dumbarton at Ibrox. Unfortunately the weather was not at all what was expected. Heavy rain had wreaked havoc with the pitch and the water had failed to drain away. Before a crowd of sixteen thousand, Celtic met an under-strength Rangers side and their superiority was in evidence almost immediately. Although Celtic were constantly threatening to score, their supporters had to wait until thirty minutes from time before they managed to put the ball in the net. They then went on to consolidate their lead by adding another almost on full-time.

That great team which brought credibility to the Irish in Scotland and gave them what Brother Walfrid had hoped for – a pride in being just who they were – were rightly celebrated wherever they went for they had won the 'treble' in what has become the true Celtic way, with skill, flair and commitment.

4

A Short Fuse

The summer of 1892 started promisingly for Doyle when he became mine host of a public house in Bellshill, another Lanarkshire mining area. No doubt wry looks were exchanged in the Everton boardroom and satisfied smiles in the Celtic one as the much-denied deal was finally completed. Doyle had one more reason to remain north of the Border. His unknown patron was undoubtedly a most generous one and probably a Celtic supporter to boot. How fortunate! For, of course, the club would not participate in such a deal.

Although Dan's footballing skills were very much in evidence by this time, his undoubted charms were not universally appreciated. Unfortunately these much-coveted talents were quite demonstrably not to the liking of the fans of Leith Athletic for some unknown reason and they showed their dislike during a five-a-side game in August of that year. Celtic were always reluctant to expose their players to the risk of injury during these somewhat meaningless tournaments – one unappreciative player described a handsome clock he'd just won as a tombstone – and they seldom sent a team. This resulted in the team that took part in the Third Lanark sports that summer showing little or no understanding of the particular strategies required, which differed greatly from those employed in a normal eleven-a-side game.

The journalist of *Scottish Sport* reported that:

> they hissed them [the Celtic] heartily as if they were the most unpopular lot in the city. Dan Doyle came in for a special dose and he, unfortunately, was foolish enough to salute the howlers on the stand with his extended digits temporarily affixed to his proboscis. Bad form even although the provocation was very strong and withal very stupid.

It wasn't the first time Doyle had thumbed his nose at critics, metaphorically or otherwise, and it most certainly wouldn't be the last although the method might vary.

The team that day was Cullen, Doyle, Dunbar, Madden and Brady and it was noted that Doyle was undoubtedly the most effective back in the tournament. Charging, tripping and badly lost tempers marked the game – tombstones could always be pawned! – which, in total, lasted twenty-five minutes. It had taken one game and three extra periods to decide the outcome. The inept but determined Celts finally lost by the only goal of the game which had come in the last few minutes. Only the defence of Cullen and Doyle had kept the team in the game at all.

Some justice was wrought for the disgraceful treatment of Doyle and, to a lesser extent, the others when Leith Athletic lost their next game, the defeat being attributed to the fierce battle with Celtic having taken its toll on them. At least the disappointed Doyle would have had some satisfaction then and he probably thought the Herculean though futile effort that the team had put in to keep the game alive had had an even more depressing effect on the Leith Athletic supporters who'd tormented them.

Although just a first-round match, it was deemed the most exciting game of the tournament. But such harassment and ridicule from the boo-boys of the day were as nothing to the bile Doyle brought upon himself in November of the same year. Thumbs and noses had obviously lost their appeal for Dan and he slipped back into the much more natural position of letting his mouth do the talking and, on the pitch, Doyle could talk up a storm.

Celtic left for Stoke at 6.10 p.m. on Sunday 6 November 1892, on the back of a 5–0 thrashing of Hearts at Parkhead. The day before, Celtic had driven 'the last nail into Hearts' League coffin and they drove it in hard and fast. All round the team is safe and sound and if there was a suspicion of certainty in football, they could be backed to sweep the board.' So opined *Scottish Sport* in November 1892. With reviews like that, the 'Greatest Team on Earth', as they were billed in Stoke, would play with no lack of confidence. Stoke had named them thus in their adverts and the whole of the Potteries looked forward to the friendly, the proceeds of which were to go to the Hanley Roman Catholic Church Building Fund.

But 'friendly' was not a word in Doyle's vocabulary when in competition. He was a fiercely motivated competitor in whichever sport he took up and the will to win often saw his side do just that often in spite of themselves. Doyle didn't suffer fools gladly on the football field. He played to his utmost and expected everyone else to do the same and he used every word in his 'workaday' vocabulary to make sure they did just that. In those days, complaints concerning foul language on the pitch were constant and one newspaper remarked that it couldn't understand why Celtic tolerated extreme foul language and displays of bad temper from two of its players. Willie Maley could still imagine, forty years later, hearing Doyle's voice ringing out all over the pitch. Celtic or Scotland team-mates got it in the neck from him – whether he was captain or not – and their finer feelings didn't matter a whit to Doyle. He was 'rugged of speech', wrote Maley of Doyle and this rather quaint euphemism fooled no one who had known the left back, especially Mr Fitzroy Norris, the English referee for the Stoke match, had he read it. There was absolutely no hint of the trouble that this game was to bring down upon Doyle's head or, in fact, the extreme humiliation the entire team would have to endure for the 'Greatest Team on Earth' was soundly beaten 5–0.

The team had been met at Crewe by the Stoke Honorary Secretary, a committeeman and one other and these three dedicated gentlemen accompanied the Celts to Stoke where they arrived at 2 a.m. In the Copeland Arms Hotel, they were served refreshments and beds awaited the tired footballers. John Glass commented afterwards that it had been the first time club officials had travelled nearly thirty miles in the dead of night to welcome the team. On reading a report of the actual game itself in Stoke's *Evening Sentinel,* the only mention of anything untoward having happened was that 'just on half-time, Doyle was cautioned for rough play'.

During the lead-up to the game, the newspaper had been full of the praises of both Celtic's charitable origins and the club's playing record. This was capped, of course, by loud admiration for the previous season's three-cup winning team. Unfortunately, Celtic were nothing short of abysmal and the Stoke supporters couldn't believe their own team's performance against a very much below-par Celtic. There is no hint at all of any major misdemeanour committed by Doyle. The only cautionary reference in the entire report is the one for rough play. The only other time his name is mentioned in the report of the game is in this paragraph:

> In the second half, a very amusing incident occurred about this time. Dunbar fouled the ball with his hand and all the Celts fell back in preparation for the free kick. To the astonishment of everybody, however, Mr Norris gave the kick to the Celts and Doyle, with his face covered in grins, took the kick.

What happened during that game involving Doyle, where his behaviour was 'abhorred by the sports writers of the day', has been used to illustrate not that Dan had a fine command of colourful, if somewhat obscene, English, but that Doyle was becoming increasingly impervious to discipline in the late 1890s. That is patently absurd as the game took place in November 1892. Doyle's behaviour on the field hardly changed at all during his entire career so the problematic discipline was, therefore, off the field. Again this did not change appreciably as he had always been a thorn in the committeemen's sides, only ever playing when he wanted to. This had been so since the beginning but, by 1897, the pressure was on the directors of the new Limited Liability Company to act in a more business-like fashion where the hired help was concerned and this triggered a change in their attitude, not in Doyle's behaviour. They should have dealt with it years before. The buck stopped with them.

However, what cannot be disputed is that his behaviour at Stoke during that game was well out of order but one wonders why none of this came out in the newspaper report of the game. As the referee's actual report to the FA is on record, his view of the matter can quite easily be known.

> In the match Stoke v Celtic, played at Stoke yesterday, D. Doyle was guilty of very bad conduct by putting up his 'fists' to an opponent and striking at him, and when I took him to task and said such behaviour would not be passed over by me and that had it not been a friendly match I would insist on his leaving the ground, he used most indecent and blasphemous language and utterly defied my power to order him off 'as he did not belong to the ****** English Association'. I then told him that I should report him to both the English and Scotch Associations and this he also blasphemously ridiculed. I had a similar trouble two or three years ago with a Scotchman at Blackburn, in a holiday match and was told then it was no

good ordering him off if he would not go as the English Association had no power to deal with Scotch offenders. I trust the law has been altered since then. I wish if it is in your power, you will take this case up against Doyle as not only was his language disgusting but at times his play against his opponents cruel and dangerous. I have not written to the Scottish Association as I am awaiting your reply which please oblige me with as soon as convenient. – Yours faithfully, Fitzroy Norris.

That evening, at a theatre outing, one of the Celtic officials expressed his disapproval of Doyle's display of temper and it resulted in a very heated dispute with Dan's friend, Jerry Reynolds. Mr Rooney, another Celtic official, however, said he thought the referee had made too much of the incident. *Scottish Sport,* commenting on this letter which they printed in its entirety, remarked that, although they didn't doubt Mr Norris was a good referee, he was not too well up on the rule book as, instead of transmitting Doyle's name and alleged offences to the SFA, Doyle's national organisation, he did so to the English one.

The leading English writer of the day, JJB of the *Sporting Chronicle,* took up the mantle of indignation and retribution with a vengeance. JJB was J. J. Bentley of Bolton Wanderers. In the summer of 1890, Doyle had told J. J. Bentley he would sign for his club but hadn't done so and had taken close season's wages from them to boot. Perhaps the relentless vendetta pursued against Doyle had some of its origins in this incident. Bentley was also hoping to be voted President of the FA some months later and so it's possible the vitriolic reactions of some newspapers were being manipulated by various factions who had their own agenda. JJB wrote:

> The Catholic charities will benefit considerably and it is a pity that such an object be marred by an exhibition of foul play and ungentlemanly behaviour on the part of D. Doyle, whose return to Scotland has not improved his temper. He was ordered off the field by Mr Norris for rough play but refused to go and not only so but made several offensive remarks about the FA and also about Mr Norris. The latter gentleman will no doubt report the matter to the FA notwithstanding Doyle's contempt for the governing body, and he will probably be suspended from playing against English clubs even if the Scottish Association is not able to deal with the matter. Such men as Doyle disgrace football.

Athletic News, commenting on the incident said:

> Doyle, as we all know, is a splendid player but is in possession of a bad temper and his refusal to obey the referee and his subsequent conduct in setting the FA at defiance, will certainly not be allowed to pass unnoticed.

Scottish Sport rushed to Dan's defence and accused Bentley of making too many sweeping conclusions and, despite agreeing that he was not incapable of rough play, asserted he was no more guilty of it than any other player. It wrote:

> Ever since his return to Scotland he has been distinguished for brilliant play, strong perhaps in texture, but never illegitimate in character. He would not have built his present great reputation as a player had he resorted to systematic rough play and bad behaviour.

It concluded its lengthy defence of the Celt with:

> Doyle, in our experience, does not, in his play, disgrace
> football, nor has he been prominent at any time for a
> display of bad temper. We therefore protest against him
> being so maligned for a fault, which, for all we know, may
> have had some excuse in provocation.

It is interesting to note the *Scottish Sport*'s view of the
game itself in November 1892 was that, except for
Cullen, Doyle, Campbell and Madden, the rest were
all non-triers. 'English pastry upset a few' was the
paper's view.

Back in the Copeland Arms Hotel, the after-match
dinner was a most cordial one with the Stoke secretary,
Mr A. Reeves, saying that they would have the greatest
pleasure fixing up future games with Celtic. They all
repaired to the Empire Theatre, Hanley, where boxes
had been reserved for them. The main complaint
against Doyle eventually crystallised into one of an
unacceptably irreverent attitude towards officialdom,
not his actual conduct towards other players on the
field. Bentley replied to the criticism of him in *Scottish
Sport* by writing that his:

> remarks were not generally about Doyle's play but his
> behaviour to the referee, to whom his language was very
> strong and indecent. His remarks about the FA were also
> in very bad taste and of a very forcible nature while the
> result is seen in Mr Norris reporting him to that body.
> There may, as *Scottish Sport* says, have been provocation
> for rough play, but I cannot see any justification for his
> remarks to the referee about the FA or the referee
> himself. Doyle was never noted for gentlemanly conduct
> whilst in England [this was the man JJB had tried so hard

to sign!] although at one period he was most unnecessarily blamed for a previous offence. At Stoke he undoubtedly lost his temper and assaulted not only the official in charge of the game but the governing body in England and for this he will unquestionably have to answer.

At this point there was a hint coming out of the hitherto silent Celtic camp as to recourse to law regarding the criticism of Doyle. In the meantime, the unrepentant Dan reappeared almost immediately in England playing for Glasgow against Sheffield. This team was comprised of players whose chances of getting a Scotland cap were still some way off if they existed at all and Doyle, as usual, took control of tactics. According to *Scottish Sport* of 15 November 1892, he was shouting at them 'to keep the ball on the floor and, taking his advice, they didn't stop till they not only equalised, but had scored a third.' The game ended in a very creditable draw, Doyle having played what *Scottish Sport* described as 'a splendid, cool game, his kicking very fine'.

By 13 December, the Stoke game had come to the fore again – this time, Doyle was being reported by the FA to the SFA for his conduct during that match. Notwithstanding the fierce newspaper criticism of Doyle, which had continued unabated, Celtic made a Christmas tour of England during which they played Ardwick (later renamed Manchester City). Celtic won 5–0 and, according to *Scottish Sport* of 30 December, 'the crowd burst into wild and prolonged demonstrations of enthusiasm and hundreds followed their brake in its progress through the streets, cheering and dancing lustily.' Doyle was in no hurry to show England a clean pair of heels for he behaved in his usual manner of remaining behind to take his own tour of his old haunts in Liverpool and Preston, along with team-mate Johnny Madden, before eventually returning to Glasgow a few days later. They were chaperoned by Tim Walls, a Celtic official. Celtic themselves were very sanguine about the criticism of their left back reckoning it was a 'quid pro quo for the dunning they had to do some time ago in order to recover a £40 guarantee'.

On 3 January 1893, it was recorded in the SFA minute book that a letter had been received from Mr Fitzroy Norris reporting Doyle for misconduct during the Stoke game. A reply to a letter written by the SFA secretary to Doyle was also read out and recorded;

Mossend, Bellshill

Sir, Your note to hand. The following is a copy of the apology which I send to Mr Norris:

Dear Sir, – Allow me to apologise and express my sincere regret for my conduct on the field at Stoke towards you. Under the excitement of the game my temper got the better of me and caused me to act in the manner I did. Hoping you will accept this – I am Yours truly

Daniel Doyle

It was a generous, though hardly grovelling, gesture indeed from Doyle, who knew just when to make the right noises in order to take the heat off and put himself in the right light. Of course, the SFA committee welcomed this magnanimous peace offering and, in their eyes, the matter was closed.

Doyle had gained the respect of all right-minded men with his latest deed of contrition and came out of it smelling of roses. But the Scottish press were hot on the heels of Fitzroy Norris and noted with glee that the SFA had instructed their secretary, Mr J. K. McDowall, to draw the FA's attention to the requirements of the laws of the game 'which evidently Mr Norris didn't know at the time of his report'. So, in the match Doyle v Referee, it was a case of Doyle 1–Referee 0! Norris's 'own goal' had allowed the Celtic back to get off more or less scot-free.

A few weeks previously, in December 1892, there was an article in *Scottish Sport*, 'How to Time a Match'. It began, 'Mr Fitzroy Norris, the English referee who didn't know how to report Doyle, endeavours in a Lancashire exchange to explain a system of time-keeping which he holds all referees should adopt.'

The Scottish newspapers weren't as forgiving as the much-maligned catalyst, Doyle, was. From another perspective, neither were the English journalists who were urging some kind of retaliation by trying to goad the FA Council into disqualifying Doyle but, wisely, that body simply allowed the matter to drop. As usual, the man from *Scottish Sport* had a word or two to say on the subject of retaliation:

> Fancy the august Council of THE Association stooping so low as to seriously notice the heated expressions of contempt poured out to a fussy and perhaps over-officious referee in a fit of temper, kindled perhaps by indiscreet threats on the part of the official directed more to him and certainly his suggestion than at the Association itself. Does not the very idea seem paltry?

This was reported on 27 January 1893, a week or so after *Pastime,* an English sports magazine, had produced a blisteringly sarcastic and grossly unfair leader devoted to Doyle and his career, an article which had Doyle, with the full backing of Celtic, considering taking legal action. The following are just a few of the comments it made.

> He is undoubtedly able to play a scrupulously fair game for he has received unsolicited testimonials to this effect from coroners' juries. On the other hand, he has certainly the power of taking care of himself in the melee, as the disasters which have befallen those who have come into collision with him amply testify.

Concerning the SFA, it stated that 'it is one of the great merits of the Scottish Committee that it is truly patriotic and impatient of dictation from foreigners. Its subjects, wherever they may be disporting themselves, may rely upon its protection.' Later, when referring to Doyle's victory over Everton, it remarked that this latest spat with authority had only yielded the bold Dan another victory. It suggested the clumsiness of the referee may have prejudiced the SFA against the complaint or they perhaps 'considered the affront committed by their countryman in a strange land a very trifling affair'. It concluded the very long, hard-hitting article thus: 'The game of football over which Associations are supposed to watch cannot fail (whatever may be the case with the lives and limbs of the players) to benefit from the patronage of such noble exponents as Mr Doyle.' In the end, their concerted efforts to have Dan punished in some tangible way by the FA failed and the matter was left to lie. Doyle himself had a copy of *Pastime* at Parkhead and was showing it to all and sundry. Little wonder there were thoughts of legal action against the magazine.

Doyle, as always, just got on with his life. Willie Maley, who was to become a close friend of Bentley, wrote years later that the cause of the estrangement between Doyle and Bentley was the fact that Doyle had let J. J. B. down badly by reneging on his promise to play for Bolton Wanderers in 1890 and that Dan was ashamed of this. In that year, Doyle had done the same thing to Celtic and yet thought nothing of renewing his friendship with the Celtic officials a short time later. In 1891, he broke his contract with Everton and returned to Scotland to play for Celtic and when Richard Molyneux, the Everton secretary, met Doyle at Celtic Park, Molyneux being in Glasgow as Everton were playing Rangers, *Scottish Sport* reported that:

> quite a number of the Everton team also turned up at Celtic Park and looked on [Celtic were playing Blackburn Rovers]. The great Everton buyer, Mr Molyneux [the man charged with signing players], who was also there, had more than a word with Doyle and the two seemed on the best of terms.

It added wryly, 'They were not left alone, however.' Celtic were aware of Everton's continuing interest in Doyle and all of this was going on whilst Doyle was about to become embroiled in legal proceedings with Everton. In another article, Willie Maley states that the three-club episode was treated as a joke by Doyle, in his usual will-o'-the-wisp manner. That he should feel so ashamed of having done less to Bolton Wanderers that he did to Everton and the guilt staying with him for years beggars belief. An educated guess would suggest Doyle blamed Bentley for constantly fuelling the fires of revenge against him at this time for his own personal gain as Bentley was indeed elected as president of the FA a few months later.

Although Doyle could quite happily take a joke against himself, being held up to national ridicule, as he had been by *Pastime*, was a very different thing for a proud man. Doyle had also been deeply affected by William Cropper's death and references to that must surely have brought back very painful memories. It has been said that Doyle never bore a grudge so perhaps none of this is as simple or transparent as it seems but the fact that he refused to dine in Bentley's company years later at a dinner in Manchester, preferring to eat alone in another room, speaks volumes about the feelings he harboured towards Bentley. Happily, though, a reconciliation was eventually effected by Willie Maley.

5

The Favourite Son

The Celtic supporters had an eternal love affair with the wayward Doyle. He was one of them, an Irish Catholic of working-class background and the wild rover all the Irish supporters liked to think mirrored their own personalities. Afraid of nothing and no one, he played hard both on and off the field and bowed to no man. This appealed greatly to the romantic notions of the displaced Irish. The first annoyance, shown when he'd played for Everton at Celtic Park in October 1889 for encouraging Darling Willie Groves to move to Everton in July of that year, according to 'Man in the Know' of the *Glasgow Observer* on 1 August 1914, had long since disappeared and Doyle's style of play brought in the crowds now following the new club.

Not only was he rightly famous for his aggressive, accurate tackling, his canny distribution of the ball and deadly free kicks, but the knowledgeable crowd also loved his intelligent play in general for this was under-pinned by an astute understanding of the game and the recognition of the need to change tactics according to the opposition. A measure of the adulation the charismatic Doyle would eventually receive from his supporters is summed up in an article (noted by James E. Handley in his book, *The Celtic Story*) which appeared in *The Irish Independent Weekly*, whose writer bemoaned the fact that the Irish in Scotland were more interested in the fortunes of Celtic than Home Rule. He wrote in his 'Glasgow Gossip' column that:

> Today we have an Irish population which are more concerned over the dumps of Doyle than the sulks of Sexton. Dillon would never be missed from the party, but Dan Doyle's absence from his club would be a national calamity.

Doyle always had a game plan to cope with the opposition he would face on any given occasion, especially in international matches. Of course, in the beginning of his Celtic career, his style occasionally lapsed and, in the game against Abercorn on 12 September 1891, he was accused of having 'a careless style and a degree of nonchalance which is carried a little too far'. That his style invariably held a degree of loftiness was perhaps Doyle's own personality revealing itself in his play. But this was, indeed, a criticism aimed at him occasionally by journalists. However, in spite of this tendency, he was named as captain of the Glasgow team against Edinburgh the following month.

Doyle's fame, of course, went wherever the Irish went and one fan from Nebraska wrote to *Scottish Sport* asking them to forward a copy of their 'Picture Gallery' containing his portrait. Such was the popularity of Dan that an advert in *Scottish Sport* of November

1894 proclaimed a broadsheet they'd produced about his life that also contained a sketch of the famous left back was having to run into several new reprints due to its popularity.

The crowds at Celtic Park loved Doyle's ability to put the wind up opposing forwards. This was mainly due to his outstanding abilities and the awe in which the opposition held him. According to *Scottish Sport*'s reporter on 22 January 1895, during a Scottish Cup defeat against Dundee that month, the nervous Cullen in goal was lucky to have 'a man like Doyle in front of him', adding:

> The latter gave a superb exhibition. Dundee's forwards hovered about him like flies round a lump of sugar, but through all he stood up to his work – a tower of strength in the face of impending disaster.

At five feet ten and twelve-and-a-half stones, Doyle wasn't easy to shift. He was a born crowd-pleaser and had his own routine at free kicks, all of which was anticipated and enjoyed by the Celtic faithful. 'Eight steps and a hitch is what Dan Doyle takes when he gives one of his exhibition place kicks. Then, as an almost invariable rule, he places the ball beautifully.' Also, if anyone moved during his run-up, he would stop dead and start all over again, frustrating the opposition even further. Doyle at times could cut up rough and his temper would come to the fore. This reporter conceded:

> On one occasion, Dan Doyle seemed fairly to lose his head and at one fell swoop cleared out a host of opponents and at the same time smashed a line flag, sent

the ball into touch and pitched poor Maley, who appeared to be getting the worst of the hard knocks that were going, sprawling over the frozen ground.

And, in January 1895, *Scottish Sport* asked the question as to whether it was greater to be a noted politician than a famous back.

Apparently, on Celtic's arrival at the station in Dundee, a huge crowd was there to greet them, all asking which man was Doyle and only dispersing when the team reached their headquarters in order to spread the news of Dan's arrival in the city. His appearance in Dundee always occasioned an outburst of hero worship from the Irish population there. When Celtic turned out at Carolina Port, Doyle was given a tremendous ovation at the end of the game. Doyle, however, did not always deserve this adulation. Willie Maley wrote of the Scottish Cup final against Queen's Park on 11 March 1893 that it was Doyle's going forward that kept the others going when all seemed lost. Unfortunately this was one game where distance and friendship obviously lent enchantment for, that day, Doyle's play was, in fact, condemned in all quarters as an uncharacteristic display of poor judgement and tactical naivety.

On a day when the game was played in a tremendous gale, Celtic found themselves 2–1 down with twenty minutes left to play. The forwards' accuracy having gone, Dan at this point decided to go centre forward and pulled Towie back into his own position. Instead of strengthening the team, it had the opposite effect. Had this come off, he would have been the hero of the day but it didn't. Doyle's desire for victory no doubt raised the supporters' hopes but the more discerning ones saw it for the error of judgement it was as it allowed a rejuvenated Queen's Park to cash in on Towie's fragility and keep a now-vulnerable Celtic defence under enormous pressure.

Doyle had begun his youthful career as a centre forward with both Rawyards and Slamannan Barnsmuir and had only adopted the role of back with Broxburn Shamrock when asked to move from centre to fill a vacancy one day. He never seemed to put aside his desire to shine in that position, forever wanting to be one of the 'glamour boys'.

The previous year, Glasgow's East End had seen people and bands parading ecstatically for their Bhoys had indeed won the Cup. This time silence reigned except for newspaper-boys calling, 'Great defeat of the Celtic – suicide of Dan Doyle!' But Doyle's efforts to secure the Cup for Celtic eventually evoked a pride in the great back and the faithful put the defeat down to rough play by Queen's Park and, of course, the referee, with one spectator opining, 'We can't expect to get Home Rule and justice on the football field in one year.'

Being idolised by the Celtic fans was something the 'one and only Dan' could rely on but it was a different case elsewhere. It was noted that, no matter if another player turned somersaults and landed on his head, only a smile would be raised but, if Doyle as much as simply lost his footing slightly, loud derisive laughter would be heard from all corners of the ground. But Doyle simply answered the bully-boys with a smile as he was 'the embodiment of good humour' (*Scottish Sport*, 19

February 1894). He had probably realised that this annoyed his tormentors more than anything else.

Doyle might have been the embodiment of good humour right enough but he was certainly no fool. As a member of the Scottish League team playing against the Football League in April 1894, Doyle was on the train taking the team south. As it passed through Bellshill, where he owned the Horse Shoe pub and where he had also recently acquired the Drill Hall in which there was another pub, a large contingent of fans waved the train on its way, all of them there as a tribute to Doyle. Shortly before, as the train had left Central Station, Glasgow, Doyle – in answer to the plea from the crowd of 'See and no' get bate [beaten]!' – had assured them that the team would do their best.

Despite his Greek-god features and terrific physique, the seductive charms of the blue-eyed, black curly-haired Dan did not blind the ladies of day from finding fault with his on-field performances. Apparently, a Celtic official and a female spectator got into an argument over Doyle's merits at the Madden benefit against Rangers in 1897 when, although the team in general hadn't played well, Doyle was regarded by the official and everyone in general as having had a good game. The result was the Celtic official was the recipient of a lawyer's letter!

Doyle's popularity was not quite universal amongst the Celtic supporters. There were a few whom he made no effort to even try to please at the beginning. A feature of Celtic's early days was the establishing of brake clubs, the forerunners of the modern Celtic supporters clubs. These clubs were made up of members of the Catholic temperance organisation, the League of the Cross. Celtic, having been constituted at a meeting in St Mary's Church Hall in Glasgow's Calton district, had a special closeness with that particular club, their colourful banner displaying a likeness of committed teetotaller Tom Maley. Dan Doyle was never a candidate for this honour as drink and Doyle were no strangers to each other even before his pub-owning days. Right from the beginning, there was underlying tension between Celtic and the brake club members. This stemmed from the fact that, not only were Celtic officials setting themselves up as publicans, they were also encouraging their players to follow them into an occupation that could lead to their own moral degradation and, by selling drink, they were exacerbating an evil which was the scourge of the working classes. *Scottish Sport* commented on 31 October 1890 that:

> on one hand, the club dispenses, with the lily hand of charity, succour to the sick and portion to the poor; on the other hand, it watches indifferently, if it does not encourage, its young men throwing themselves recklessly into a business of which every tendency is towards moral ruin.

Celtic had always denied that they were the means of Doyle becoming the licensee of the pub in Bellshill but this denial of having a hand in it, officially or otherwise, fooled no one. At the club's AGM of 1894, according to the *Scottish Referee*, a Mr J. O'Donohoe asked what the liability was to the club of retaining Dan Doyle. John Glass replied that it was £2 a week, the same as the other players. When the same questioner asked if it were true that they'd purchased the building for Doyle in which his business was situated, there were loud cries of 'Next business!' from those present. Mr Glass could be heard among the raised voices saying that he'd answered the question. So, £2 a week it was.

But, by July 1897, the *Glasgow Examiner* reported that, at a meeting of the Celtic brake clubs, it was said that the brake clubs were in the invidious position of being members of the League of the Cross and, as such, they were supporting temperance on one hand and brewers and publicans on the other by purchasing season tickets for Parkhead. The resentment had been added to by Celtic's refusal to give reductions on the season tickets that they insisted had been promised to them by a Celtic official.

Doyle was not the first Celtic player by any means to harbour hopes of becoming a publican. Willie Groves had been refused a licence for a pub in Glasgow's Taylor Street in 1890 for no other reason than that he was a footballer and it was implied that such men were a bunch of rogues and vagabonds. Another twist to the brake clubs versus Doyle saga came in the form of Father David Murie, a curate at St Mary's, who was also the League's spiritual director there and the cleric pilloried in the *North British Daily Mail* in November/December 1894 by some members of St Mary's League of the Cross for, in their eyes, inflicting on them a president who was most unsuitable for that position. The dispute between some members and Father Murie had come to a head at that time concerning the election of a president of the League who was an insurance agent by day and, on Saturday evenings, helped serve drink in a public house. The members concluded that this gentleman had been thrust upon them by a curate variously described as intolerant, headstrong, narrow-minded and tyrannical. Relations between Father Murie and the League members had obviously broken down quite dramatically.

The curate countered with the assertion that there was nothing in the rules to stop this and, in his opinion, the League, like the Church, was open to all. This serious breech was compounded by the fact that the letters were published in the *North British Daily Mail*, a newspaper which had apparently once referred to temperance workers as 'night soil'. The *Glasgow Observer*, with its close connections to the Catholic Church, receiving the letters first, had refused to publish them and subsequently regretted this decision as it meant the matter was being ventilated in the *North British Daily Mail*, a secular newspaper.

Whatever the rights and wrongs of the matter, Father Murie became the recipient of Dan Doyle's Charity Cup winner's medal of 1895. The story behind the medal is that it was given by Dan to Father Murie, his nephew. I have been unable to verify from official documents this family relationship between the two men, but it's perfectly possible they were related in some way. Both were born in 1864, Doyle in Paisley and Father Murie (Murrie on his birth certificate) in Airdrie where most of Doyle's relatives lived. Father Murie's own father was a miner as were most of the Doyles and Dan subsequently became one himself at his home village of Rawyards, near Airdrie. David

Murie's father then changed jobs to that of publican and, when he died at an early age, Father Murie's mother remarried and her new husband took over the running of the pub. Hence, Father Murie and Dan Doyle had a great deal in common as far as background was concerned.

When Doyle first signed for Celtic in 1891, he lived in Marlborough Street, not a stone's throw from St Mary's. Father Murie was already noted on the 1891 census as being a priest there and what man would understand the hard drinking and heavy gambling legacy of Doyle's mining background better than the headstrong curate who exhibited more than one Doyle trait? The Glasgow Charity Cup medal won by Doyle came as a result of beating Rangers 4–0 in the 1895 final.

Father Murie was no more liked by his temperance parishioners than Doyle was. For some reason, possibly because he was never slow to show his contempt for anyone trying to tell him what to do or how to behave, Doyle riled some of the St Mary members more than the other Celtic publicans. But *Scottish Sport* noted on 15 April 1898 that 'Dan Doyle has gifted a billiard table to the League of the Cross. Dan doesn't bear malice towards opponents.' (Doyle, who was quite an accomplished billiards player, at one time arranged a match between himself and the Scottish champion in Bellshill, eight hundred being the winning score with Doyle being gifted four hundred. Unfortunately, there is no note of how the game went. He also arranged a match between the League of the Cross and four Celtic players, Doyle, Welford, Storrier and Crossan, in which the Celtic team were triumphant.) There is also no doubt that Doyle gave the spirited curate the medal and apparently it was in 1895 that Father Murie was transferred from St Mary's to Johnstone so the medal was perhaps a farewell gift from one renegade to another. The medal is on loan to the Visitor Centre at Celtic Park and it was as a result of pure curiosity to find out more about that beautiful medal, when I first started my job as a guide there, that this book has come about.

The columns of the *Glasgow Observer* were constantly filled with letters from the League of the Cross concerning Celtic and publicans and, at times, the spirit merchants of Celtic must have felt under siege. But, by 1897, there were enough of them to console each other – namely, James Kelly, James Grant, James and William McKillop, John O'Hara, Michael Dunbar, Paddy Gallacher, J. H. McLaughlin and Dan Doyle. At no time does Doyle appear on the lists of those present, including Celtic players, at League socials and an educated guess would have to conclude he wouldn't have been welcome. In fact, although several Celtic players, who were friends of Doyle, were the main providers of the musical input at socials, Doyle is conspicuously absent at such events, excepting those where only the players and Celtic officials would get together after matches. Doyle was more at home where gambling in the form of cards and billiard matches were the order of the day.

On a different note, an amusing piece was printed in *Scottish Sport* on 16 October 1893.

They talk of the Queen's Park lady supporter! Why, the Celtic have dozens. The familiar – almost affectionate way – some of the ladies on the stand at Celtic Park spoke of Jerry, Tommy, Sandy, Joey and the others was most refreshing.

If Doyle was included in 'the others', he was obviously not one of the main attractions. Perhaps the handsome Doyle, the essence of working-class masculinity, was a little too dangerous for the more genteel 'standites'.

The ordinary supporters' affection for the temperamental and unpredictable Doyle never wavered. They knew, as did the players, that the 'black curly-haired giant was a fighter from head to heel', according to 'Brigadier' (*Daily Record and Mail*, 11 September, 1935) and that was all they asked of the Airdrie lad.

6

A Controversial Man

'It is probable that the Celtic will formulate a charge to the League concerning the treatment of their players at Paisley on Saturday.' – so it was reported in the *Scottish Sport* on 14 February 1893 after the fiasco when Celtic played Abercorn at Underwood. Abercorn were fresh from a series of defeats culminating in a complete collapse when playing Third Lanark in a cup tie. Always great crowd-pullers, the Celts sallied into town ready for action, having attracted five thousand spectators, the biggest crowd of the season, to Underwood Park, a mere mile from Doyle's birthplace. But, for some reason, Paisley never claimed him as its own and he most certainly made no bones about considering himself an Airdrie lad.

A scorching pace marked the game throughout and the Abercorn supporters readied themselves to witness their team being blown away only to find their worst nightmare turn into their best-case scenario as Abercorn quickly went two goals up. But, five minutes later, it was all square and the inevitable collapse would surely follow as Celtic produced some brilliant play, penning the home team well into their own half. Unfortunately for the Celts, Abercorn began by playing a blinder and this, coupled with the Celtic forwards' shooting now being ineffectual, saw the Parkhead Bhoys go in 3–2 down at half-time.

The second half brought the home team yet another goal and, despite Doyle trying some long shots and Kelly doing his level best to salvage something from the game, the referee's whistle finally put the seal on Celtic's misery. It was generally agreed at the time that, although it was a great game, the best team did not win. Celtic's dribbling and passing were regarded as very fine but, yet again, the old complaint held true – they overdid the fancy work although every one of their players put in sterling work.

The final whistle signalled a pitch invasion by the Abercorn supporters and they carried their team shoulder high. 'A Puffer' of *Scottish Sport* reported that, on the Saturday night, whilst in Glasgow with some cyclist friends, Johnny Madden, the Celtic centre forward appeared and gave him a graphic account of what the Celtic players had had to contend with at Underwood at full-time. He himself had been struck on the face with a stick while Reynolds, Doyle and some others had received blows, 'Dan being fairly lifted off his feet'. The Celts had to fight their way into the pavilion, Doyle eventually managing to lead them there.

When the affair came before the SFA in March 1893, Mr Eaglesham of Abercorn stated that the entire affair was Doyle's fault as he had knocked down and kicked a boy who had passed some remark to him and the gallant Abercorn supporters had rushed to the boy's rescue. He also asked why, in Celtic's complaint, there was no mention of Jerry Reynolds. In the police office, Reynolds had been accused by an Abercorn supporter of assault, the charges only being withdrawn in deference to Reynolds' wife who was dangerously ill and on assurances from John Glass that he'd make recompense for the damage done to the man's clothing, loss of teeth etc. Apparently Celtic were now refusing to honour this magnanimous gesture. The lack of proper policing was also denied.

The police superintendent's letter was read next and, in it, he stated that, by the end of the game, one sergeant and six constables were in attendance. He also stated that, during the evening, a charge was lodged against one of the Celtic players but, after some conversation and a denial of the charge, the Celtic man – who was unnamed – agreed to give the Paisley man a new vest in lieu of the one damaged by blood. No mention of teeth!

Since the Celtic complaint was that Abercorn had not taken proper precautions for the safety of the visiting team, the SFA decided they had first to prove an assault had taken place. They had nothing to do with free fights amongst spectators on the field apparently. Mr Curtis of Celtic stated that he had personally seen the passage to the pavilion blocked by spectators, Campbell caught by the throat and Kelly, Doyle and Madden also receiving injuries – perhaps it was just as well Abercorn had won! He remarked that the Abercorn committee were conspicuous by their absence. He also had not seen any Celtic player going in and then coming out of the pavilion again in order to sort out the boy with the unfortunate big mouth.

Johnny Campbell was the next witness and he told of being attacked by two men and being caught by the throat. He'd also seen a man jump off the grand-stand and chase Madden with a stick. (Madden had apparently remarked, 'You'd think you'd won the Scottish Cup!')

'What did you do when you were attacked?' Campbell was asked.

'What could I do?'

'I don't know.'

'Neither do I.'

That piece of cross-examination obviously helped a lot!

Campbell blamed the whole sorry episode on an Abercorn player who roared at the top of his voice when they were winning, 'I don't think that is becoming for a sportsman.' He also maintained no Celtic player left the dressing room once they'd all reached it and that they all left together.

Doyle was there to give evidence but the Committee decided that Mr Goudie of Abercorn should be heard next. He stated that either Doyle or Reynolds had caused the row by coming out of the pavilion, crossing the track and striking a little boy – although he admitted he didn't actually see anything like that happening. He also didn't see any of the Celts being 'ill-used' – they might have been but he didn't see it. (One wonders why he was called as a witness at all.)

Asked why the police had been ordered to gather round the pavilion at the close of a match, Mr Goudie reluctantly stated that 'once or twice they had had little rows with spectators interfering with the referee and the police were there to protect them'. Abercorn were infamous for the threatening behaviour of their supporters towards visiting teams and officials. The chairman of the SFA committee continued questioning Mr Goudie of Abercorn, saying, 'How did you know it was one of the backs?'

'The others were on the field.'

'What about the goalkeeper?'

'It was not the goalkeeper.'

'Of course, you know Doyle and Reynolds?'

'Yes, very well – but I could not say which one committed the assault.'

This was probably because he hadn't seen the alleged assault happen. After the referee's report in which he stated he saw nothing – no doubt he'd taken to his heels the minute he'd blown the whistle, wise man – it was suggested that the vital point was whether or not one of the Celtic players had gone into the pavilion and come out again. The chairman said that it didn't matter a whit if this had happened half-a-dozen times – the question was whether or not Abercorn had made proper provision for the safety of the visiting team. A motion that Abercorn had taken every precaution for the safety of the visiting team was carried and an amendment that they hadn't was defeated by twelve votes to four. Dan Doyle never gave evidence.

There was a more peaceful outcome to a typical Dan Doyle performance when, on 17 November 1894,

Celtic met Rangers at Cathkin Park in the final of the Glasgow Cup, a cup that had been fiercely fought over since its inception. The holders were Rangers but things looked good for the Celts when McMahon won the toss and elected to play with the blustering wind behind his team. The team was well prepared for the game, their training having been much more vigorous than usual. Most of the players like Madden and Reynolds who had previously been on the injured list were now relatively sound and Doyle – 'a braver back never presented a broader chest to the enemy' – had even finished up his training with a round or two of the track which he hadn't done since the international in April when he'd captained the Scotland team against England.

The game itself got off to a great start and gave every indication of a great final to come but, unfortunately, it flattered to deceive. Fortunately for Celtic, goalkeeper McArthur was the man of the match and managed to thwart the brilliant play of the Rangers forwards time and time again as the Celtic team in front of him fell apart. It looked as if it was going to be Doyle's worst day as he was repeatedly beaten and his kicking, too, was somewhat below par. But, when the chips were really down, Dan, as always, came into his own. Despite a generally poor first-half showing, his free kick, after thirty minutes, resulted in a hotly disputed goal, the referee being swamped by players crowding and gesticulating. This goal was quickly followed by another one from John Divers and the Bhoys went in at half-time two goals up.

When adversity was coming their way, Rangers in no way exhibited the same fighting qualities of the

Celts, simply 'throwing in the sponge' when the going got really rough, according to the *Scottish Sport's* reporter on 20 November 1894.

Celtic had lost McMahon after twenty-five minutes and Willie Maley was lame throughout the last hour but they held on magnificently and won the Glasgow Cup for the third time. The game was reckoned to be a hard, trying ordeal in which the Celts produced the stamina required to come out winners. There were twenty thousand spectators at the match, a good number coming from the towns and villages of Lanarkshire in dog carts. A more astute commentator concluded that the gruelling which both teams had taken wouldn't enhance their chances of beating the next team on their fixture list although he also noted that Celtic had come out of it worse.

The formal dinner after the match was held in the players' favourite venue, the Alexandra Hotel, and, at it, a Rangers official stated that Doyle, McEleny and McArthur had been great obstacles in the way of Rangers' success.

The Celts then drove home to a fitting heroes' welcome at Celtic Park. Before arriving at the stadium, they called in at Willie Maley's outfitter's shop in the Gallowgate. Maley had announced in advance that, should the result go Celtic's way, the team would drop by his shop and, in anticipation of this, when they got to the Gallowgate a crowd had gathered to see the trophy. At the reception at Celtic Park, John Glass, the first speaker, congratulated the committee on selecting such a fine team and ended with an apt tribute to Jerry Reynolds, who had so recently been injured.

The Scotland team that played England in 1895 – (back row) Drummond, Lambie, Russell and Gibson; (front row) Gulliland, Simpson, Waddell, Oswald (captain), McPherson, Doyle and McArthur. Doyle famously went AWOL for the twenty-four hours preceding the match, only turning up an hour before kick-off. He received a tremendous ovation from the Liverpool Irish when he took to the field. England won 3-0.

This mug commemorating England v Scotland games was issued in the early 1900s and depicts the most famous of the internationalists. It shows Dan Doyle and the English winger, Billy Bassett.

Doyle was capped eight times for Scotland and captained the side in a 2-2 draw against England in April 1894 at Celtic Park. At times, the action on the pitch that day could hardly be seen because of thick smoke drifting in from the nearby brickworks.

The Everton team of season 1889/90 – (back row) D. Waugh (trainer), A. Hannah (captain), R. E. Smalley, D. Doyle and R. Molyneux (secretary); (middle row) A. Latta, J. Weir, J. Holt, G. Farmer and E. Chadwick; (front row) C. Parry, F. Geary and A. Brady. The team were runners-up in the league that season.

The Everton team of season 1890/91 – (back row) D. Waugh (trainer), R. Stockton (umpire), A Hannah (captain), J. Angus, D. Doyle and R. Molyneux (secretary); (middle row) A. Latta, D. Kirkwood, J. Holt, W. Campbell and A. Millward; (front row) A. Brady, F. Geary and E. Chadwick. This team won the League Championship – Everton's first-ever league title. Alec Brady, who came to Celtic with Doyle in 1891, was in both of these teams.

The Celtic League Championship-wining side of season 1895/96 – (back row) J. Blessington, B. Battles, P. Meehan, player's name unknown, A. Martin and W. Ferguson; (front row) D. McArthur, J. Madden, J. Kelly, A. McMahon, D. Doyle and W. Maley.

This rare photograph was taken shortly after the 'strike' of 28 November 1896 and shows Doyle behind the man with the ball and Willie Groves seated on the far right. Willie was brought back from Hibernian to bolster the team when the trio who went on strike were suspended but he managed only two games for Celtic before his health broke down.

65

This form of 1889 shows both Dan Doyle and Willie Groves registered as Everton players. Unlike Doyle, Willie had an almost immediate change of heart and, with the help of Tom Maley, was reinstated as an amateur in Scotland in order to play, once more, for Celtic.

This is another rare example of an official document. It shows Doyle was 'whitewashed' on Everton's players' registration form for season 1891/92. He had been reinstated as an amateur in Scotland and had signed for Celtic.

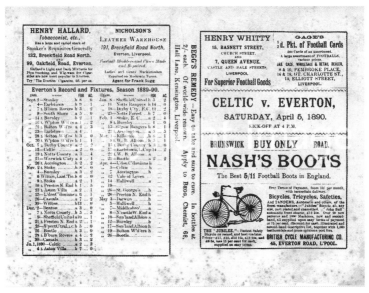

These pages from a rare programme show Everton's fixture list and results for the season 1889/90 and an advert for the Everton v Celtic match on 5 April 1890.
(reproduced by kind permission of Paul Hendry)

CELTIC TEAM.

Referee—Mr. Cooper   Umpire—

Goal
McLaughlin

Right Back   *Left Back*
Reynolds   McKeown

Half Backs
Gallacher   Maley   Dowds

Right Wing   *Left Wing*
Madden   Dunbar   Gallacher   Coleman

Centre
Campbell

Centre
Hammond

Left Wing   *Right Wing*
Milward   Chadwick   Brady   Latta

Half Backs
Parry   Holt   Kirkwood

Left Back   *Right Back*
Doyle   Hannah

Goal
Smalley

Umpire—Mr. Stockton

EVERTON TEAM.

Here are the Everton and Celtic line-ups for that game. Doyle is at left back for Everton with Alec Brady at inside right. This also shows the legendary fullback pairing of Hannah and Doyle. Doyle had already played alongside many of the Celtic team during his days at Hibernian.

(reproduced by kind permission of Paul Hendry)

J. Campbell

This is Doyle's Celtic team-mate Johnny Campbell. A very skilful player, he formed a legendary partnership with Sandy McMahon on the left wing. In 1892, like Doyle, he was a member of the first Celtic team to win the Scottish Cup.

D. DOYLE.

This photograph of Dan Doyle was taken during the highly successful season of 1895/96 when Celtic won the League Championship, the Glasgow Cup and the Glasgow Charity Cup.

Doyle has the ball at his feet in this Celtic team photograph. Dating from March 1898, it is unusual in that it was taken just before a kick-off. The game was against Sheffield United and it was dubbed the 'Championship of Great Britain'. Celtic lost the match but, as Sheffield United had not actually won their league championship at the time the game was played, it was judged to have been a 'premature' description anyway.

This Celtic squad of 1897/98 won the league for the fourth time without losing a single match. It was in November of this season that Doyle had a very public 'strike' of his own with the directors of the new limited liability company that was now Celtic.

A rare action photograph, this was taken on 25 May 1895 when Celtic won the Glasgow Charity Cup, beating Rangers 4-0 in the final at Cathkin 'Old' Park. The team that day was McArthur, Meehan, Doyle, O'Rourke, Kelly, McEleny, Morrison, Madden, McMahon, Divers and Ferguson.

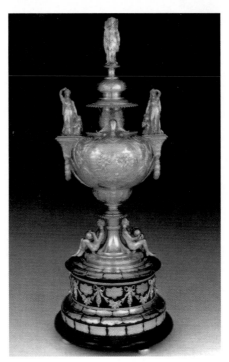

The Glasgow Charity Cup was always fiercely contested and, with that win over Rangers in 1895, Celtic had taken the trophy four times in a row.

This is the Glasgow Charity Cup medal which Doyle won in 1895, following Celtic's 4-0 victory over Rangers. The reverse shows Doyle's name engraved on what must be one of the most beautiful sporting medals ever made. He presented the medal to Fr Murie of St Mary's, Abercromby Street, Glasgow. St Mary's hall was where Celtic FC had been founded in November 1887.
(reproduced by kind permission of Kevin McDade)

Not to be outdone as regards this tribute, *Scottish Sport* reported that:

> Doyle got on his pins. Much was expected of Dan after his brilliant generalship on the field. Nor were we disappointed. With modest mien and humble speech, Dan started. The house was hushed. Never did minister of the realm rise in important debate under more favourable auspices. Pointing in the direction of George Square, he said that were he [Reynolds] but twenty-five years of age, he could raise as much money with his football talents as would erect the Municipal Buildings all over again!

It was a fine tribute to his friend from a man who had put a shipyard valuation, the Mersey Docks, on his own ability! What went down well with reporters was the fact that pleasantness seemed to have finally returned to the meetings of the two teams, extreme unpleasantness among the players having marred recent games. This was attributed by some newspapers to religious differences but the Celtic players vehemently denied this and blamed the actions of one of the Rangers team in a previous match for it. The players' version is almost certainly the correct one as, less than a year later, Celtic were already fielding four Protestants in the team. On 16 March, *Scottish Sport* had reported that there 'is no truth in the story we have heard circulated to the effect that Celtic allowed Hearts to win the game last Saturday in order to deprive Rangers of second place.' The social at the Alexandra Hotel afforded an opportunity for peace to break out after the bad feelings which had been very much in evidence during their last league encounter.

Another memorable game in Doyle's career has to be the only game, apart from the Stoke friendly, when he was ordered off. In May 1893, Celtic were already champions and, in the closing game of the league, they were soundly beaten 5–2 by Third Lanark, a team they had already defeated many times that season. An excuse for Celtic's poor performance could have been that they had played and beaten Dumbarton in a charity match the previous evening. They had also been without stalwarts Reynolds, Maley and McMahon. It was a Queen's birthday holiday match and it was noted that Doyle was 'conspicuous for his loyalty to the Crown' (*Scottish Sport*, 23 May 1893) by agreeing to take a holiday from his work at the referee's request!

The play in general was not of the highest order. Johnstone of the Thirds had the crowd at Celtic Park incensed by his persistent fouling of Kelly and Doyle and, although Doyle complained to the referee and in fact told him he'd sort out Johnstone himself if he got no protection from him, the official continued to turn a blind eye. Dan was as good as his word and was ordered off for it. He was duly reported by Referee McNicol to the SFA for kicking an opponent.

At the SFA disciplinary meeting, Doyle had no compunction in owning up to the offence he'd committed – described by the referee as hacking – saying that he'd received severe provocation. The upshot of it all was that Doyle, according to the SFA minutes of 20 July 1893, was suspended until 31 August and an amendment that he be only censured was defeated by nine votes to four.

It has been written elsewhere that Doyle did not start for Celtic on several occasions until after the season had begun, the implication being that he had gone AWOL. This suspension in season 1893/94 was obviously for that reason – despite the fact that he was training with the team early in August. In 1895, although he had played for J. H. McLaughlin's Celtic Cricket Club during the close season, by the start of the new season, Doyle was unavailable to play as he was suffering from quinsy, an abscess in the back of the throat, a condition which recurred on numerous occasions during his career.

On leaving the SFA's Carlton Place committee rooms, Doyle was asked by reporters what the outcome had been.

'A month,' said Doyle, 'and it's me and the Celts who have built this place.' He was, of course, referring to the palatial SFA headquarters.

One of the most notorious episodes in the history of Celtic must surely be that which took place on 28 November 1896. Three of the team were refusing to play unless certain pressmen, whom the players considered were victimising them, were ejected from the press box. There was a dressing-room fracas over this and it resulted in Doyle having to lead a ten-man team on to the field at Parkhead to play what could have been a league championship decider. At that time, Hibernian were heading the table with Celtic running a close second. The Hibs team, who were already on the pitch, looked fighting fit and the lengthy delay in the match kicking off caused the supporters to begin to become irritated. Their foot-stamping turned to anxiety as they realised that, if a Celtic team did manage to turn out at all, it was obviously going to be a makeshift one.

Eventually, when the Celtic players came out, it was 'in broken detachments' and they numbered only ten – which, incidentally, when the whistle blew, Hibs failed to notice. Of these ten, only eight were first-team regulars. They were augmented by Barney Crossan and Willie Maley who partnered Doyle at the back. Fielding those two plus having a man missing must have sounded alarm bells for the supporters and a frantic scramble by the press ensued to find out what calamity had befallen the club to force the committee into putting out such a team when it was probably already known that Meehan, Battles and Divers were in the dressing-room.

Hibs should have buried that team but, in fact, the makeshift Celts fought for their lives in probably the greatest display of unrelenting courage of any team before or since. They were one up with three minutes remaining and looked likely to pull off a great victory. By this time, they were buoyed up by the appearance of Tom Dunbar who had been hurried over by cab from playing in a reserve game at Hampden to take Willie Maley's place at the back. This had allowed Maley to go forward to fill the vacant spot.

Unfortunately for Celtic, Martin of Hibs shot from twenty-five yards out and, through a tangle of legs, the ball found the net and Hibs salvaged a draw from the 'erratic, unorthodox and unflinching Celts' (*Scottish Sport*, 1 December 1896). John H. McLaughlin wrote that the makeshift team that day stood not only between Celtic and the extinction of league hopes, but nearly dug a grave for Hibs' hopes as well. According to the sports writers present, McArthur in goal was superb, Doyle and Kelly magnificent, Russell and King grand and Crossan and Ferguson unflinching. The legendary fighting qualities of Celtic teams when their backs were to the wall were enshrined forever in the players who took the field that day at Parkhead. Doyle led the side superbly, as he always did when having to claw his and the team's way out of adversity, but it is to the eternal credit of these men that the potentially disastrous events of the dressing-room revolt were not allowed to distract their minds from the game in hand.

The Celtic forward line in particular had come in for some pretty vitriolic criticism in the press during the weeks leading up to the game and this obviously had an unsettling effect on the players who watched as their committee were apparently content to let them take any flak the sports writers cared to throw at them. That they should choose the moment of stripping for the match to demand that the Celtic officials clear the press box of the representatives of the *Scottish Umpire* and the *Scottish Referee* before they would play that day, had a catastrophic effect on their own careers for, of course, there was no way the officials could be seen to give in to what was virtually blackmail.

The officials made grandiloquent speeches about 'freedom of the press' but it was really this challenge to their own authority that it was all about. They did agree that a great injustice was being done to the players and promised to take it up with the journalists concerned and their newspapers but Battles, Meehan and Divers, the three who'd refused to play, would not accept this and wanted immediate action. They were suspended for the season at a meeting of the club's officials and their wages reduced to 2/6d per week.

Apart from the playing difficulties this brought to the club, who were the innocent party in all this, Celtic also had the additional worry that another team, English or Scottish, might pay those players in secret for the rest of the season and then sign them. But this scenario was a by-product of their own actions and one that should have been thought through before any decisions had been made. Thus both team and players were distinct losers. No matter what sympathy their comrades might have for them, the Celts were on a £10 bonus if they won the league and that was quite evidently not now going to happen with a seriously weakened team.

In September 1931, 'Veteran' of the *Evening Times*, wrote that he was the only outsider in the dressing room that day and he knew exactly what had happened. He stated that the team had sat around the stove in the dressing room discussing the fierce, sustained attack on them and it was suggested that they threaten to strike if the culprits weren't removed from the press box. Battles, Meehan and Divers warmed to the idea but, when the trainer looked in and told them to get ready, the player who had made the original suggestion got stripped first. 'Veteran' called this a cowardly act but wouldn't reveal the name of the player. He didn't consider that it might just have been a throwaway line.

A Celtic player, Jimmy Blessington, later said that the three had made up their minds some time previous to that day and had told no one. He also said that no arguments could change their minds and they redressed. It has also been suggested that at least two of the three strikers already had offers from English teams and were trying to 'work their passage'. Captain of the team Doyle was present and a £10 bonus was probably more than enough for him not to contemplate striking. Willie Maley wrote of him that if ever a man had the courage of his convictions, it was Doyle.

Doyle had been through a lot worse at the hands of the English press, concerning his dealings with Everton and on his own, to let a few bad press reports put his position in jeopardy. As we've already learned, Doyle was subjected to national ridicule in 1893 by *Pastime* but did nothing concrete about it. Such was his faith in himself that people's opinions mattered very little to him in the long run. He was too pragmatic to force himself into a corner, where the exit route was strictly to his disadvantage. Nor was he ever described as cowardly and he always remained good friends with the strikers who at no point blamed anyone else for their actions.

To say that working-class men would virtually throw away their livelihoods on a whim does a disservice to these men's intelligence. Even if the consequences were more dire than they'd anticipated, they must surely have been aware of the importance of the game and also the grave risk of holding the club to ransom so openly. Doyle had done it time and time again but had always known when it was in his best interests to compromise. Why his three team-mates continued with their threats remains a mystery. John McLaughlin posed the question that many had asked: were there hidden reasons behind the players' actions? According to McLaughlin, the players, when formally interviewed by the club's officials, insisted there weren't. He described himself as an eyewitness and told of the players being stripped and ready to take the field when they issued their ultimatum. He said:

> The proceedings, although short, got extremely stormy and language was used of a description that doesn't bear retelling. The faithful eight went on the field, while Messrs Maley and Crossan stripped and a messenger was sent to Hampden to capture Tommy Dunbar and bring him over.

A photographer had been engaged to capture both teams but the Celtic one was not taken. McLaughlin regretted that it had been a great opportunity lost to put the personnel of an eleven 'of whom the club may well be proud' on record. Doyle had been pilloried on many occasions not only by opposing spectators but also by the press but he always managed to maintain good relations with them. He no doubt sympathised with the strikers but Doyle's lifelong ability to see the bigger picture probably swung into action and he came out smelling of roses yet again. As captain that day and one of the most verbally volatile players at the club, his forthright contribution would no doubt have been one of those whose language so shocked John McLaughlin.

Blessington suggested that the three had not told the others of their intentions. The reason could simply have been that they knew the others wouldn't join them merely to have one set of reporters martyred in the eyes of the others, thus bringing even more grief upon their heads. It's also a reasonable suggestion that some of the verbal dissent that rang out came from the others with the bonus in mind. They'd fought long and hard for it and now it was being thrown away. Whatever it was, eight of the regulars did play that day along with three others and Doyle played his heart out. That he subsequently played a major part in Celtic's Scottish Cup downfall some six weeks later is an entirely different matter.

The 'strike' match fiasco was in stark contrast to an event a year earlier at the same venue when, in October 1895, Celtic inflicted the most crushing defeat of the day upon Dundee, beating that team which was fresh from victories over Hearts and Rangers to the tune of 11–0 – Celtic's record victory. Unfortunately for Dundee, a crowd of eleven thousand had turned up to see the match. Celtic had their strongest team out whilst Dundee was short of their experienced captain Hendry and a youngster called Ferrier was pitched in to take his place. It had been snowing overnight but this seemed to make watching the game more pleasant, the temperature having risen slightly.

The Celts were no sooner on the pitch than they had to return to the pavilion to change their colours owing to the similarity of their stripes to Dundee's. It would be interesting to know what the alternative strip was. There was no sign of the nightmare that was about to befall the visitors as straight away they bore down on the home goal and had an unsuccessful attempt at scoring. For the first ten minutes or so, everything went Dundee's way except for the brilliance of Doyle and his partner thwarting them at the last hurdle. Then gradually Celtic's forwards got going. By the time twenty minutes had elapsed, Celtic had taken control and their domination was so complete, the crowd wondered how on earth the Dundee team could possibly have beaten Hearts 5–0. With Maley, Kelly and Battles holding the Dundee forwards easily, the Dundee threat was reduced not only to a minimum but very nearly to extinction. Everyone had been eager to see Dundee's new 'wonder boy', Vail of Lochgelly, but his appearance only left the spectators wondering how he'd earned his reputation. Perhaps the occasion was too much for him as it was the first time he'd played in a big match in Glasgow.

Blessington opened the scoring for Celtic and the others followed his lead, the forwards that day being simply 'phenomenal'. At half-time, Celtic were leading 6–0. A catalogue of accidents marked the second half, with Barney Battles falling so hard he received a head injury and was off the field for some time. In the first half, Longair of Dundee, in attempting to head the ball, had got a knock on the side of his head which left him completely dazed and, with his eyesight affected, he had to go off. Not only did he fail to reappear for the second half but he was kept company in the dressing room by young Ferrier who had injured his ankle. Evidently medical opinion was that Longair was suffering from concussion. Thus Dundee had to play out the game with only nine men and it was agreed that they played better with these nine than when they had eleven. However, they lost another five goals and thus retired at full-time with the score 11–0 against them, Doyle scoring one.

Dundee were obviously very handicapped in the game by losing two players but they were up against an inspired Celtic and the 6–0 half-time score must testify to that. Several Dundee officials gave their opinions of the game, remarking that they'd never seen Celtic so deadly. The Dundee linesman – each side provided a linesman in those days – stated that the team was brilliant in every department and Keillor, the Dundee forward, said, somewhat sourly, that Celtic had got all the breaks – all eleven of them! Nobody asked Barrett, the Dundee goalkeeper, what he thought of his appalling defence but his injured captain, Hendry, who had been unfit for the match, gave his opinion of Barrett in two words – dead off!

Sandy McMahon commented that he felt as fresh as a daisy at the end of the match and Dan Doyle's comments and opinions were, as always, sought out after the game. 'Another record! Delighted at having a hand in the pie. Thought of having a shy on the right wing with Meechan in the second half.' Breaking and making records were what the Parkhead faithful were now coming to expect and the players were more than happy to oblige with the 'great and only Dan' obviously still harbouring those secret longings of a career nearer the opposition's goal.

7

Manipulation's the Name of the Game

Dan Doyle was a very likeable person and, despite his excessive bossiness on the pitch, he remained a firm favourite with his team-mates. Whenever Celtic played friendlies in England, Doyle would invariably remain behind with one or two of the others and spend time looking up old friends from his playing days there. This satisfied two needs – that of enjoying the company of old friends and also keeping him in the know as to what was happening in footballing circles. Knowledge was power and nobody knew that better than Doyle. Being in control was like a drug to him, no matter how trivial the situation might be. But he made and kept friends very easily and, indeed, his old team-mate, Andrew Hannah, with whom he'd formed the great Everton defence in the Championship-winning side of 1890/91 which was deemed the essence of fearlessness, was to be one of a small band who gathered in Dalbeth Cemetery, Glasgow, in April 1918 for Doyle's funeral.

Doyle's arrival at Celtic Park in 1891 caused the players already there to ask for more money and, the following season, it was Doyle himself who did the negotiations with John Glass on their behalf, albeit unsuccessfully. Doyle was an inveterate gambler and in this he was not alone among the Celtic players. He would bet on anything and his prowess at cards was legendary. He had a great sense of humour but it almost invariably involved some form of gambling, however small the stakes.

Even when he was about to take part in a match against Hearts at Tynecastle, he was to be found amusing all in the pavilion. As Dan provided the entertainment in the form of the popular 'three slices a penny' game where his gold watch was the prize and coppers were the stakes, the laughter from his team-mates could be heard by the people entering the ground. Doyle, needless to say, pocketed a handful of coins and nobody else got the watch.

It was quite common at that time for players to bet on their own team winning and Doyle liked nothing better than to bet with an individual forward as to how many that man would score in a particular match. After the 8–0 defeat of Partick Thistle in November 1892, it was reported that at least one Celtic player had an interest in the score reaching double figures. It was said that Doyle religiously attended the big athletic meetings in Glasgow and the Celtic players were frequently seen in each other's company on these occasions and the like where betting was a major activity. In 1897 some of the leading players for the club were involved in some serious betting (and losing) at the horseracing. *Scottish Sport,* on 17 September 1897, without naming anyone, reported that 'players of credit and renown have been absent from their training quarters this week. Have the Ayr races had anything to do with this?'

On a trip to London, Doyle, it was reported, came down the grand staircase of the team hotel dressed 'for once' in a well-fitting, navy-blue suit and sat himself down amongst the gentlemen there, lighting up one of his favourite Havanas. Sitting with one leg crossed over the other, he was showing a rather eccentric striped sock which the newspapermen present couldn't help but comment on. Doyle was approached by one young reporter who viewed this Scotsman as one who was rather naive, if not pretty thick, and duly commented on the fashion faux pas. This, of course, was the whole point of the exercise and Dan reeled in his prey. He bet the young Londoner that he couldn't find another of its kind in the whole of London and the youngster took the bet, £10 being the stake. As Doyle had anticipated, the journalist pointed to Doyle's other foot which, on inspection, was not clothed in the other striped sock – instead, Doyle had put on a black cashmere one.

All of his pranks revolved around betting and, naturally, the other Celts usually came off worst as he regularly beat them at cards and billiards. Doyle, Reynolds, Madden and McMahon were frequently seen in each other's company whether at athletics meetings or at other types of sports meetings. In June of 1893, the Celts were well represented at the Howe

Cycling Club Sports, with Cullen, Reynolds, Doyle and McMahon among those present.

In April of the same year, *Scottish Sport*'s man reported:

> The Sunderland players were spectators at the Celtic–Everton match and the Celts were in evidence at Ibrox on Wednesday. Doyle, Madden, Reynolds, T. Dunbar and McMahon were perched together at the west corner of the pavilion and it was interesting to hear their observations on the incidents which cropped up. Reynolds assumed the role of joker but Gallacher (the old Celtic player) was a match for him.

A large contingent of Celtic players, including Doyle, turned up at Barrowfield, the ground of Clyde FC, to watch the British Ladies FC play and Jerry Reynolds provided the blistering and none too complimentary running commentary on the game – Jerry was famed for his somewhat acerbic wit! This was the same ground where, in February 1895, Doyle, Dan McArthur and Willie Maley were seen to be spectators at the Clyde v St Bernard's match as the Celtic v Dundee game had been postponed. During the game, McArthur had the misfortune to have his pocket picked which resulted in the thief being thirty shillings better off at the end of the match.

Doyle was, without doubt, an inspirational captain of both Celtic and Scotland. He was officially Celtic's captain both in season 1895/96 and 1896/97. In January 1896, he was seen at Cathkin Park sizing up the opposition for the forthcoming Scottish Cup tie, due to be played on the eighteenth of that month, and he was looking very serious. What he saw must have pleased him for the rumour in Glasgow was that the Celtic players had backed themselves to win at 4 to 1 on.

The minute Doyle stepped on to the pitch, everyone was fair game, friend or not. In March 1896, during a Glasgow league game against Rangers, Jimmy Blessington hurt his knee badly and left the field. Doyle immediately bawled over to the pavilion to send him back out and, after a rub-down, that's exactly what happened.

Of course, in those days the captain's word was law on the field and it was he who dictated tactics – a heavy burden indeed as the buck stopped with him. Doyle was probably only ever convinced of a man's need to quit if he had broken his leg in one or two very obvious places. If Doyle led by example, as indeed he did on the field, he must surely have seen his own goalkeeper follow this to the letter. Still, during a match versus Hearts in October 1896, he lectured Dan McArthur like a schoolboy in front of thousands of spectators for failing to save a penalty. This was generally considered to be 'bad form' by the sports writers but such criticism mattered nothing to Doyle.

Dan Doyle was at no point in his life very far removed from miners and their families and playing football for a living was, for him, just a walk in the park compared with the hellish jobs that those miners he served and listened to in his two pubs in Bellshill had to endure on a daily basis. During the international trials of 1896, both Doyle and Madden were playing, this time in opposing teams, and the crowd thought that Madden, who was really making up the numbers in the 'C' team as opposed to Doyle in the 'A' team, was out to do his friend Doyle a favour by not giving him a hard time. They frequently and sarcastically called out to Madden, 'Pass to Doyle!' The newspapers were equally derisive saying that Madden eventually played well when he realised he too was in the game. This was complete nonsense as both men were highly competitive and near the end of the game, when Madden brought Dan down to 'Mother Earth', Doyle gave him a salutary lecture for doing so.

Doyle had persuaded Madden and another Celtic man, Divers, to leave the Celts with him in June 1895. This caused consternation all round but it was only a temporary transfer to Dykehead in Lanarkshire in order to play in the Airdrie charity games and Doyle and Divers were duly transferred back to Celtic a month later – although there is no trace of Madden's transfer to Dykehead at SFA headquarters.

Doyle was forever persuading Celtic to take strong teams out to Mossend to play some of his local teams and it seems everyone wanted to take part as a great time was generally had by all.

There is no doubt that Doyle led the Celtic committeemen a merry dance but, given how he had behaved towards their Everton counterparts, they should have been on their guard – but were they? The fact that he did as he liked almost his entire career at Parkhead – and virtually played when he wanted to from the start probably – answers that question. The annual re-signing of players invariably saw Doyle becoming the last to put pen to paper. The reporter for

Scottish Sport took time out on 16 June 1896 to give this a bit of psychological probing:

> Doyle has never been too quick to re-sign. If he has not been the last of the pack each season to adhibit his signature, he has been about the last. Others besides the Parkhead officials have observed the reluctance and some of them in their self-sufficient sapiency have not hesitated to formulate a theory to explain it. The most common is, of course, the one that any yokel could hazard without the expenditure of a halfpenny worth of brains – that Dan has something special in his eye every time; either a new sphere of usefulness in another club or an increase in his screw. Of course there may be other reasons. He may enjoy the fun of keeping the officials in politic suspense or it is even possible that he may have serious thoughts of at last carrying out his long-announced intention of retiring. One Parkhead official, with a wicked twinkle in his eye, suggested that Dan was meditating amateurism and his only fear was that, if he carried out that deep design, he might go over to the Queen's Park!

Doyle had a great influence over the players, captain or not, which was very simply demonstrated in January 1895. The team was supposed to play Dundee in a Scottish Cup tie and were breakfasting in The Mikado, a restaurant in Jamaica Street, Glasgow, before travelling to the east coast. Two of the Celtic officials, Messrs Curtis and Gallacher, had gone to Dundee the previous evening to look after the club's interests and while the team were in the restaurant, a wire was received stating that the referee had declared the ground unplayable. A further communication came a short time later asking the Celts to still travel and play a friendly. 'No cup tie, no friendly,' said Doyle and a chorus of 'amens' followed. The team did not go.

The saga of Doyle versus the directors was minutely reported in the sports press in December 1897, a year after the three-player strike. This time the crisis at Parkhead saw Doyle centre stage. Having bossed them around for as long as he'd been there, the directors, now answerable to shareholders, had had enough and decided to flex their collective muscles. The teams that they'd selected for the games against Hibs and Third Lanark had both included Dan at left back. Evidently the directors had decreed thus, the newspapers had followed suit and the world and his wife had agreed – but Doyle didn't. There was going to be no Doyle playing against Hibs that day.

This was nothing new as, on many occasions, Doyle had turned up and refused to strip – he'd done so in 1894 against Third Lanark in a Charity Cup game. That time, Doyle had evidently not travelled to Hampden with Celtic but he was there anyway. He was asked to strip when he arrived but refused. In another game, this time against Hearts in November of the same year, he sauntered in at the last minute and declared himself ready to play and, although Jerry Reynolds was already stripped and ready, Doyle played.

Scottish Sport's reporter takes up the story in an article in December 1897.

At Edinburgh, with admirable self-abnegation, Welford, who was under doctor's orders not to play for a fortnight, stripped and filled the vacancy caused by the inexcusable absence of Doyle. The committee sympathised with

Welford at the time and, after the match, he was granted a fortnight's holiday which we may say in passing was well-deserved. Welford went away immediately to Stockton to enjoy himself amongst friends. On Friday last, however, he received a telegram requesting him to come back if he could, and, bruised and battered and stiffened as he was, to sacrifice himself as those who saw his breakdown on Saturday can say.

All this was due to Doyle being 'in the sulks'. Having been fined £5 for not turning up to the Hibs match, Dan refused to strip against Third Lanark until the fine had been remitted. The directors refused and Doyle didn't strip. The contingency plan was that, if Jim Welford couldn't make it, George Allan would play. Welford did make it but, unfortunately, he broke down during the match. This was the last straw and the directors, who were raging at Doyle for having brought about this situation for no great reason, decided to reaffirm who was in charge. Doyle, as usual, had his backers among them but, this time, their influence did not hold sway. Doyle was telling his side of the story to one and all and insisting that this had all happened before – as, indeed, it had – and that the fines were always remitted and peace would reign once more in Paradise.

The pre-Limited Liability Company committee naturally vigorously denied any such thing had happened before and no solution seemed in sight for the new directors were not a committee responsible for a charity. Celtic had become a Limited Liability Company earlier in the year. The men Doyle was now dealing with had been elected as directors of the company in June 1897 and they were now answerable to the shareholders. They had resolved to let one and all, especially the wayward Dan, know who now ruled the roost and they were determined to ram home the message that whoever paid the piper called the tune.

Celtic Park was a hive of meetings every day, the main topic being Doyle and his defiance which, really, the men in charge at Parkhead had visited upon themselves by kowtowing for years to the massive ego that was Doyle's. His bargaining strategy had always been a fatal mixture of threats and irresistible charm and the men at the top had fallen for it year in, year out. Everyone awaited with bated breath the ultimatum that would surely come from the corridors of Parkhead. After a prolonged meeting on 10 December 1897, the directors let it be known that, no matter what, they were not giving in. The football was well and truly in the left back's part of the pitch.

All this naturally posed the question as to whether or not Celtic could do without Doyle. A writer in *Scottish Sport* reckoned that, although at some time they would have to due to his advancing years, Celtic were currently far better with Doyle than without him and cited the recent series of games with Rangers where his influence had been paramount, his play splendid and his judgement supreme. At the same time, nobody thought that the directors should 'surrender to the reckless whim or the defiant insubordination of any player simply because he happens to be a tower of strength'.

Everyone was hoping that it could be settled amicably and quickly – especially the Parkhead faithful, who had no desire whatever to lose the 'one and only Dan'. The matter was finally resolved in a game against Partick Thistle when all eyes were on the pavilion to see whether or not Doyle had decided to turn out once more for Celtic. And, as the players came out, there he was as large as life and smiling philosophically to himself. Doyle was nobody's fool and, as a gambler of long standing, he knew when he didn't hold the winning hand. The firmness of the directors had paid off and their reducing the fine to just one game was probably enough to satisfy honour all round.

The Celtic management took great care of their players and Doyle was very friendly with the committeemen who were very approachable anyway. Doyle got his own way most of the time but not always in verbal duels. When writing John H. McLaughlin's obituary in the *Glasgow Observer* of 21 August 1909, Tom Maley noted that, one night, McLaughlin, who was the Celtic chairman of the day, and Doyle were having some good-natured banter.

> Said the chairman: 'I have had a turn at every place at the disposal of Celtic members save playing and, on your display today, Dan, I can start anytime at that.' Dan, a bit nettled retorted: 'There's one place you have not been tried and that's the gate.' At once, J. H. retorted: 'Not so fast. That's about the first place they put me, so that I would be able to pay a lot of you amateurs!

The players were frequently taken to the theatre to relax after a match and sometimes they even went after training. Before big games, the team was invariably taken to a resort on the Clyde where brisk walks and a bit of sprinting were the order of the day. Sometimes it was Rothesay and sometimes Millport, the latter being McLaughlin's favourite holiday spot. If the weather was good, they all took to rowing boats and, on one occasion, one of the lug boats went missing for a while in the Firth of Clyde so, when the gloriously gifted Jimmy Johnstone found himself in the same metaphorical boat some seventy or so years later, he was simply following the tradition set by those Celts of yore.

Of course, it wasn't only the boats that disappeared. Doyle himself was a frequent sinner in this respect and he would do so without resorting to the connivance of the Clyde. After a visit by the team to play a friendly in Newcastle in September 1895, Doyle, Cullen, McManus and McMahon decided to stay on for a short time. *Scottish Sport* takes up the story:

> There is a wealth of talent at Parkhead this season and this quartette thought they'd never be missed and an extra day or two was neither here nor there. Of course, they were quite aware of the fact that the club had two engagements to fulfil on Saturday and that it was a case of all hands on deck. The non-arrival of the quartette in Glasgow on Friday landed the club in a difficulty as Doyle and McMahon were in the League eleven to oppose Rangers, while McManus and Cullen were in the team v Motherwell (a charity match to be played on 6 September).

The missing four did not appear in time to play and the Motherwell game had to be cancelled. When they finally did appear, they were fined and Doyle and McMahon were suspended for the following game, giving the club an even bigger headache as they were already badly off for players due to injuries.

Doyle took his duties when on the field extremely seriously but he had a deplorable lack of any sense of responsibility at all other times. This weathervane style of thinking seemed to be an uncontrollable part of him – if he bothered to try to control it at all. Going absent was something he did at various points in his career and this was coupled with the fact that, when he did turn up, it was he who decided at the last minute whether or not he was going to play.

His most famous disappearing act was when he failed to turn up for the Scottish Cup tie with Arthurlie in January 1897, just a few weeks after he'd played heroically in the match against Hibs when three of the team went on strike. The day before the game with Arthurlie at Barrhead, the papers were saying that Doyle was thinking of taking a turn at right back. Arthurlie were very small beer and the result was a forgone conclusion as, even in their own league, they'd done nothing. If life is too short to stuff a mushroom, then, for Doyle, it was definitely too short for him to be bothered helping to stuff Arthurlie and he just got on with living – Celtic having found it impossible to track him down. Although he was fined for his outrageously selfish and unprofessional behaviour, it's interesting to note that, a week later, it was reported that he was still not quite fit. No further elucidation of this was apparently forthcoming in any subsequent reports.

Unfortunately, Celtic were having injury problems and this, plus the lack of their three strikers, meant the Parkhead Bhoys couldn't come up with more than a few regulars to face the minnows that day. The

Arthurlie boys were definitely not class acts but, where their feet failed them, their brains didn't and, by narrowing the pitch in a bid to negate Celtic's playing style's need for space, they hit the jackpot and Celtic's Cup hopes were relegated to the bin. Doyle took most of the flak for the defeat. His Celtic career is littered with newspaper comments on how the Celtic committeemen were delighted when he showed up unexpectedly and announced he was going to play or they were wondering if he could be 'prevailed upon to play'. Yet, for some reason, they never lost patience with him – probably because, when he did play, he could make any team look good.

8

Pure Inspiration

Doyle's international career was a glittering one, regardless of the success – or lack of it – of the teams in which he played. He was also a great favourite with the press for his readiness to give his opinions on tactics and the merits of players and, in turn, the press greatly valued his judgement. Thus we have on record his own assessment of some of the international teams in which he played and the teams he played against.

Doyle's signing for Celtic immediately made him eligible to play for Scotland as, at that time, no Anglos were selected for the international team. Indeed, as far back as 1884, an SFA committee had been set up to blacklist Anglos, as the Scottish players playing in England were called. In an article in *Scottish Sport* in October 1893, a journalist wrote that hero worship of players had been around for some time and all sorts of questions were sent into the paper concerning topics such as height, weight, size of boots, who cuts their hair etc., proving that the more things change, the more they stay the same! The team at that time which was the object of most adulation was Celtic. The journalist, on finding the Celtic team having tea at one of their favourite restaurants, The Mikado, put controversial questions to some of the team. These questions were concerning the nationality of the Celtic players and there had been great controversy amongst the readers regarding this manifestation of anti-Irish-Catholic feeling.

'Is the Celtic football team composed entirely of Irishmen?'

'Yes, all Irishmen.'

'If so, why is it some of them are asked to play for Scotland in international matches?'

'Because, although Irish by parentage, they are Scottish by birth and, therefore, eligible to play in international matches.'

'What is an Irishman?'

'Give up. Ask Arthur J. Balfour, Dan Doyle, John Morley and Jerry Reynolds.' [Balfour and Morley were both MPs heavily involved in the Irish Home Rule debate.]

'Could you name any player of the first eleven whose claim to be an Irishman could be disputed?'

'No and we would advise our correspondent not to try it. The Celts are too powerful kickers to dispute with.'

An Edinburgh critic, writing to the same paper, protested against the number of Celtic players – six – in the international trial sides. 'Surely we can find eleven Scotsmen to represent us without having to call in the aid of Irishmen, whether born in Scotland or elsewhere?'

Scottish Sport's reply condemned the letter as 'savouring of sectarianism and bigotry. The club is a Scottish club, their players have been born and bred in Scotland and in every respect they are as fully qualified to participate in the event as any Mac that may be placed.' All this in 1893!

In another article, they refused to tell 'Curious, Paisley' anything about the players' religion or want of it, commenting that 'the Celts would be as good footballers were they Mormons'.

Doyle, in fact, played for Scotland five times against England, twice against Ireland, once against Wales and eight times for the Scottish League team.

Before the actual representative team was selected, trial matches were held where four teams competed for places against the other three Home countries, the strongest being chosen for the England match. These games were something of a farce as the A team was obviously the one to play against England no matter how badly a fancied player played on that day. Although games at no time influenced the final selection and were the subject of mounting criticism, they were great money-spinners for the SFA and, as such, were not likely to be abolished for some considerable time.

In 1895, Doyle was severely criticised for his performance and the *Glasgow Observer*'s 'Celt' remarked that:

> Doyle's culpably stupid display of cocky indifference not only stultified his own somewhat battered reputation but also placed McArthur (the Celtic goalkeeper) in a most unenviable position. Doyle's abilities are not so superlatively pre-eminent nor is his England cap so secure that

he can afford to make himself the butt of every gadding idler with a turn for sarcasm. We have no hesitation in saying that on the day's display, his place in the order of merit was 44th and that there were dozens of players round the ropes who could have filled the position more creditably than he.

It was also noted in the same newspaper that the Celtic officials 'seemed terribly annoyed at Doyle's fifth-rate display in the trials'. However, 'Celt' finished his article by suggesting the best team to face the English and, of course, Doyle was at left back! This display was a repeat of the one in 1892 when Dan's loftiness was once more in evidence, his performance 'being good enough for a common or garden back but, for the great and only Dan, he was, like a few more, out of it. His misses were far too numerous to come from a class back.'

Doyle's first international appearance was against England at Ibrox on 2 April 1892. Scottish fans had a somewhat optimistic view that this team might beat England but unfortunately it was not to be – the team was outplayed and outclassed in every position except those of Doyle and left half Mitchell. Scotland went down 4–1 and it's interesting to note that, despite his abysmal display in the trials, Doyle was one of the few successes despite being played out of position at right back. *The Scotsman* reported on 4 April 1892 that it was to Doyle that credit was due for the fact that the defeat wasn't heavier.

For his first international against England, he kept his head in a losing game in a manner which would have done credit to a much more experienced player and it's no exaggeration to say he was the best man on the field. For a great part of the second half, he was simply impassable and, with feet and head, put in an immense amount of work, a good deal of which was in the way of retrieving mistakes of his comrades.

Doyle came through the ordeal of having to perform out-of-form back Arnott's work as well as his own with flying colours. Despite playing against England five times, Doyle was destined to be on the winning side only once.

The following year it seems that Doyle did not show his usual disregard for the opposition and any selector who might be watching but, rather, displayed what the onlookers hoped was simply a temporary loss of confidence. A week previously, he'd had a good game against Queen's Park in the first of the two games that were the Scottish Cup final of 1893, the second match resulting from the first one having been declared a 'friendly'. The second was postponed until after the international trials had taken place.

Doyle was not selected to play against England which was probably just as well considering the ominous remark in *Pastime* that the English players were looking forward to meeting him. Then again, perhaps the writer of that article was putting the intelligence of footballers in general merely at the level of his own. It had been written in one of the Scottish papers in 1890 that, in turning down Willie Groves' application for a licence for a Glasgow public house for no great reason, the Licensing Board was implying that footballers were incapable of conducting legitimate business. For whatever reason, Doyle's confidence seemed to have deserted him, which was quite a problem for a man whose life turned on his own high opinion of himself, so, whether it was, in fact, a lack of confidence or, indeed, a lack of concentration is not known. Consequently, due to this lack of form, he was more or less relegated to playing in the Wales game in March at Wrexham.

Dan, the perennial wild rover, loved going on the spree and being part of a team where only two players were not from either Queen's Park or his own Celtic helped to make up for only being selected for a minor international and not for the main one against England. The players, as usual, settled down as best they could to the train journey with J. K. McDowall, secretary of the SFA, presiding over the team as they played cards and, of course, the 'bank' was in J. K. McDowall's care 'but Dan Doyle, as usual, asserted his authority and soon transferred the latter into his pocket while his partner, Robert Foyers, slept the sleep of the just' (*Scottish Sport,* 21 March 1893).

The reception at Blossom's Hotel in Chester couldn't have been better and the 'pretty whimpers of the parlourmaids' were much appreciated by one and all, it seems – especially Doyle for it was reported in *Scottish Sport* on 21 March 1893 that 'Doyle said he couldn't help being a good-looking fellow as an apology for worming his way into the affections of one of the girls as soon as he arrived'. He was unmarried at this time and was extremely attractive to the opposite sex so it was probably a natural reaction to the 'pretty whimpers'.

Despite Doyle having quite a few uncharacteristic lapses which put the hearts of the newspapermen firmly in their mouths and being totally eclipsed by Foyers, Scotland's other back, the team managed to beat Wales at Wrexham 8–0. Unfortunately Doyle was once more played out of position at right back. He was picked for the Scottish League team versus the Football League later that month and happily his form was back to normal as he had a great game whilst being watched as to how he'd fare against the English crack, Bassett. Dan rose to the occasion as he almost always did when in the spotlight and played 'in splendid style' (*Scottish Sport*, 11 April 1893). William Bassett was to become the preferred opposition for Doyle when playing against England and he could handle him well.

1894 saw Doyle make an effort in the trials for the first time and a cap against England was his by a mile, his berth being described as a mortal certainty. This time the venue was Celtic Park and he was captain by right instead of by force of personality. Doyle habitually acted as if he were captain on all other occasions. A crowd of forty thousand turned up hoping to see England get a thorough drubbing. Nothing changes! Doyle was forever giving interviews, his opinions eagerly canvassed by the sports journalists of the day and the man from *Scottish Sport* was no exception, giving us, at this great distance in time from the actual event, Doyle's opinions in his own words.

The views expressed by prominent players on International topics are always worth careful consideration. In the interchange of opinion on comparative form they view matters from a player's standpoint and judge form on practical experiences in club matches.

'Well, Dan, what do you think of our prospects this year?' we remarked to Doyle of the Celtic the other day when the conversation had turned on the trial selections.

With a shake of the head the burly Celt hit the point at once and with characteristic frankness said, 'We're quite able to lick England if the men wouldn't funk, but they go on the field shaking in their shoes at the bare idea of opposing an English team. That's my experience of International elevens in Scotland, and I don't wonder at our defeats.'

'And what's your opinion of a Scottish team for April 7th?' we queried further.

'Much depends on the forwards,' he responded promptly. 'The three inside players selected with a view to combination will do the trick and we have them all in Glasgow too. My idea, after carefully weighing all the candidates up, would be Blessington, outside right with W. Lambie backing him up, Sandy McMahon in the centre and Johnnie McPherson partnering Campbell. There you are,' he says, 'and let the boys turn out as if a club cup tie was at stake and the thing's moleskin. Ta-ta! There goes my train!'

And, a few seconds later, the Scotsman with the greatest experience of English play was ensconced in a comfortable smoking carriage en route to Mossend.

Doyle was very fond of a mild Havana.

The naming of the team and Doyle as captain saw Celtic provide its third captain of a Scottish International team against England since the club was formed in 1888, the others being James McLaren and James Kelly. Doyle declared himself fairly well satisfied with the composition of the team he was to lead although he would have preferred that Adams should have partnered Isaac Begbie as he reckoned these two men provided a most successful partnership but he still thought Scotland would win. Doyle also wanted the 'three forwards to play the inside game' which he had great faith in. Dan considered that, against an English side, wing play would only ruin any chances Scotland might have.

He was also in favour of having a quiet practice some afternoon with the Roamers providing the opposition. Willie Maley also played for, and was indeed a founding member of, the Roamers, an amateur team who were more than happy to give International teams and the like a practice game. Before the game, Doyle's views were naturally sought by journalists wanting to know how he thought the International would go and Dan, as usual, was only too happy to oblige, as this extract from *Scottish Sport*, 6 April 1894, shows:

> 'Much will depend on the first fifteen minutes play and the steadiness and the placing of the Scottish halfbacks. The forwards can only beat England at her own game and that is by the three inside men unselfishly combining together and the wing forwards lying well up for the pass.'

Doyle was satisfied that the Scots could 'wipe the Rose if the team go in with stout hearts and with the pluck for which Scotsmen are famous'. He truly believed Scotland could win this time.

John Glass, the Celtic president, was also asked for his views and, in the same edition of *Scottish Sport*, he declared:

I have three hats on Scotland (Doyle, Blessington and McMahon) and there you are. Great faith in Doyle's judgment and ability and think that with even a moderate partner, a defence which included Dan, would not be weak. Don't consider Sillars weak. Expect Celtic contingent will be a success.

The game was a sell-out – 'bung full' – and displaced pressmen had to seek refuge from the crowded barricades by sitting on a fence in front of the pavilion. However, every time they popped up to watch the game, they were showered with handfuls of gravel. This crushing caused several accidents and some people had to be taken to the Royal Infirmary to have their injuries treated. The view of the game was not helped by the fact that thick smoke tended to waft over the ground from the nearby brickworks. Doyle had his men turn out on to the field early in order to put in some five minutes kicking practice.

Dan's taking of the first free kick against England for a foul was said to have him placing the ball as carefully as a golfer set his tee. Evidently Doyle expected great things to come of this free kick as he spat on his hands and tucked up his sleeves before placing the ball. With all eyes on him and everyone holding his breath, Dan managed to send the ball high over the bar. However, whoever had selected Doyle as captain must have been proud for not only was his individual play regarded as superlative in containing Goodall and Bassett but his captaincy had never been bettered against England. When, in the first part of the match, England swung into action magnificently, it was then that Doyle's great powers of skill and leadership came into their own and he went 'into the struggle with heart and soul' (*Scottish Sport*, 9 April 1894).

The result was a 2–2 draw but Scotland were unlucky not to win, according to Brian James in his 1968 book, *England versus Scotland*. Scotland were the more workmanlike side and had taken the lead with a brilliant Lambie goal. England were a very good side and 'with a less experienced man than Doyle, the English right wing would have proved deadly' (*Scottish Sport*, 9 April 1894). Doyle's method of toppling Goodall over the touchline caused great amusement among the Scotland supporters but it was also noted that 'the great back' (*Scottish Sport*, 9 April 1894) didn't always come off best.

It was generally agreed that the difference between the sides was the Scottish defence and much was owed to Doyle's brilliant captaincy. John Goodall was the England captain and it was generally held that both teams were captained by Scotsmen, Goodall's family hailing from Ayrshire. Incidentally, each of England's players was presented with an umbrella by a Scottish manufacturer.

The after-match dinner was held at the Alexandra Hotel in Glasgow, the usual place for these events. There were no ladies present which left the men to get up to whatever shenanigans they liked to indulge in. There were the usual toasts, with Mr Sliman of the SFA rising to propose the toast to 'The Teams'. *Scottish Sport*'s man was there to record it, with the following words appearing in the edition of 9 April 1894:

Mr Sliman passed on to couple the toast with the name of Mr Doyle – and then what a shout there was. In the highest terms of praise did Mr Sliman speak. He was the giant, the player amongst players and the players amongst the twenty-two who had disported themselves. Such were the eulogies passed on Daniel. The toast, with its 'attachment', was enthusiastically dealt with, Highland honours being given. Amidst great cheering, Doyle replied in a few well-chosen words of thanks and with a quiet determined expression, said he hoped Scotland would be on the winning side next year. Doyle was enthusiastically cheered on resuming his chair.

The English view of Doyle was that he was now a better player than he had been with Everton and he had performed brilliantly during the game. The downside of this for Celtic was that Doyle was again firmly in the sights of English clubs and on their 'most wanted' lists, with Everton more determined than ever to get their left back once more domiciled in Liverpool. The Celtic players then joined the rest of the Celtic team in England where Celtic were touring at this time. However, Doyle didn't play as he had injured his knee slightly in the International and so he contented himself with spectating.

Celtic's boardroom must have been a place of mixed emotions when they realised that the game between the Football League and the Scottish League, with Doyle a member of the visiting team, was being played at Everton's ground, Goodison Park. Doyle, of course, in his time with Everton had never played there as Anfield had been the team's home ground at that time. Season 1891/92 was Everton's last at Anfield. In the early spring of that year, there had been a row between

Everton and the club's landlord over the rent – not an unfamiliar story to Celtic – and the majority of the Everton membership decided to move to Goodison Park. Those remaining formed a new club, Liverpool.

The hard-working *Scottish Sport* reporter, who judged Doyle knew the English game better than most, asked Dan his opinion on the forthcoming game. As Doyle had played in all these League representative matches so far, he would have a good idea of what was likely to happen. He also noted, accurately as it turned out, that Doyle was sure to get a terrific reception from the Everton supporters. Their conversation appeared in *Scottish Sport* on 20 April 1894.

> 'Well, Doyle,' we queried after settling down for a smoke, 'what cheer for Scotland on Saturday?'
>
> 'The best,' he replied with a grin and a nod of the head. 'There's only one way. Let the men go bang into the game with the determination to win. If they go into the game with the same spirit as the Association team against England did at Celtic Park, then we can win, but it will be a hard job all the same. I don't think I ever saw a Scottish team against England show such great fighting and the League can do the same now.'
>
> 'What's your opinion regarding the English and Scottish teams?' we asked.
>
> 'I should say both teams are slightly weaker than the recent Association teams but that's got to be demonstrated yet. A lot as you know depends on how you go into a game.'
>
> 'Wherein, think you, our men can improve?' (*sic*)
>
> 'I have often said to our men at Parkhead, a great deal depends on the halfbacks. Crack English halfbacks lie

between the inside men or not far out in order to intercept the pass. If they collar the pass, they show their opponents they're there to spoil their tactics and the result is the enemy are compelled to play this game. We forced England to do this at Parkhead and had them play to a standstill. Bad luck alone kept us from winning.'

'Do you think, Dan, Scotland can win?' we further queried.

'Yes, if we force them to play a wing game, we can lick them out of the shop. I expect very equal play, lots of excitement and a hard game. You can bet,' he said in conclusion, accompanying the remark with a merry twinkle of his eye, 'a coal pit to a bottle of gum on Scotland winning if we are winning by two goals to none four minutes from the finish.'

Dan therefore got his third League cap in succession. The selectors were anxious that the team would turn out in peak condition and so it was decided that they would travel down to Liverpool on the Friday afternoon. The team and officials met at The Mikado and 'partook of Mr Lee's appealing fare' (*Scottish Sport*, 23 April 1894). The railway authorities had placed two saloons at their disposal and everyone soon settled in to pass the five hours. Apparently railway travel was supposed to be something of an art but it was decided that it was, with footballers, a fine art as, within minutes, hats and boots had been removed and caps and slippers were their visible replacements.

Doyle and the team had been sent off in style by a crowd of several hundred supporters at Glasgow's Central Station, all urging them to victory. Doyle, forever willing to acknowledge the burden placed upon their footballing heroes by the adoring crowds, bowed seriously and assured them that the team would do their best. Daily life was hard and bleak for most of the Celtic supporters and Doyle knew from personal experience what joy a victory for the national representatives, as much as one for Celtic, could bring to the grinding existence of ordinary people. Doyle had been there himself and never forgot his roots.

On the journey south, they saw a rugby match in progress at Lancaster, the maul being a tight one. The general opinion was that Doyle and Begbie could have shifted the lot!

Twenty-five thousand spectators turned up to see the game and, when the Scottish team eventually came out ten minutes late, Doyle received 'the warmest of welcomes from the Liverpudlians both at the start and at half-time' (*Scottish Sport*, 23 April 1894). The Scotsmen had hoped to improve upon the Parkhead result but had to content themselves with a draw. It was deemed a sterling match of a very high standard, with Adams and Doyle being in 'slashing form'.

From the Celtic point of view, the most worrying aspect was that, when Doyle and Richard Molyneux, the Everton scalp-hunter, met, 'it was like Livingstone and Stanley all over' (*Scottish Sport*, 23 April 1894).

Later that evening, when the team were back at their hotel, a big cheer went up when the result of the Celtic v Aston Villa match for the unofficial British Championship was made known. 'The Celtic contingent threw themselves into each other's arms and danced for joy.' (All quoted material from *Scottish Sport*, 23 April 1894.)

On 8 February 1895, it was reported that Dan Doyle had already begun special training in order to gain his cap against England. The extra training plus Celtic's new stand on fining those who didn't turn up for training obviously paid off as he was selected for both the England and Ireland Internationals and for the match against the Football League.

The Irish one came up first on 30 March at Celtic Park and once again, Doyle was played at right back. Before a crowd of fifteen thousand, Scotland defeated Ireland 3–1 despite a performance which was not exactly vintage. The entire defence was rated disappointing, with 'Doyle no more his old self than an old hack is like a Derby winner', according to *Scottish Sport* on 2 April 1895 – a comment which was sure to get the man with more than a passing interest in horse racing riled and fired up.

Scottish Sport's reporter was obviously an admirer of Foyers as he advocated that Doyle should be played out of position again against England in order to accommodate Foyers. But the selectors did not agree and Dan found himself nominated at left back to partner John Drummond in a match that was to take him back to Goodison Park once more.

There was a great deal of interest in the game and special trains were laid on from Glasgow both on the evening before and on the morning of the game. The team, however, was considered weak and not much hope was invested in a victory. Scotland's chances of emerging the winner had been substantially diminished by the inexplicable exclusion of Celtic's McMahon which left just two other Celts, Doyle and

McArthur, to face the foe. Apparently one of the selectors jokingly advocated the trial of a number of lady footballers who had made their debut in London a few days previously if the Scottish team failed to get a result.

The team was given a great send-off, every space on the platform and every inch of the booking-hall being packed with well-wishers. Each player had to run the gauntlet, being cheered and greeted as they did so, some looking suitably modest – but there was no Doyle. This time the dining car and two saloons had been allocated to the party and, in one of the saloons, the selection committee had gathered to discuss the possibility that Dan wouldn't turn up. Rumours abounded that he'd decided not to. This possibility hadn't escaped the crowd and they were beginning to get restless as time went by without the one and only Dan appearing to take his cheers in his usual avuncular fashion. The selectors had already got Foyers standing by just in case Doyle was a no-show.

But, while they debated amongst themselves, a tremendous cheer went up as the popular Celt appeared, looking fit as a fiddle, smiling broadly and accompanied by A. Kirkwood of the Scottish League. Kirkwood was eventually to become Vice-President of the SFA and he was another of those fiery Lanarkshire individuals so beloved of Doyle. It was, therefore, no surprise that they were great friends.

The only other cause for anxiety on the journey south was an apparent lack of water in the saloon. The SFA secretary, J. K. McDowall, ordered the train to be stopped as it was impossible to contemplate a trip as far as Liverpool without water. His vigorous language was evidently enough to prove to officials he wasn't a man to be trifled with and water was soon to hand, much to the relief of both teetotallers and non-teetotallers alike for very different reasons.

In many accounts of this game, Doyle is named as the team's captain but, of course, it was simply Dan taking control again and being allowed to do so. This was the International where Scotland reputedly lost her captain but didn't – instead, she simply misplaced her left back. Doyle disappeared almost as soon as the team checked into their hotel on the Friday afternoon and, by noon, the following day – the day of the match – he was still missing. Despite the Scottish officials scouring the whole of Liverpool, he was nowhere to be found. When Doyle didn't want to be found, there was no power on earth that could change that, as Celtic knew to their cost. Foyers was drafted in and had already stripped for action when the bould Dan sallied in an hour before kick-off. In those days, teams generally stripped and visited the photographer's before proceeding to the game and naturally the photograph of the Scotland team versus England of 1895 shows the handsome Dan taking his rightful place in the picture as no one had the nerve to tell him he'd been substituted!

Dan's explanation for his absence was that he'd spent the night with some friends from his Everton days and some reports claim that, when he did appear, one of the Everton players was with him. Some idea of what he actually did for part of that evening comes from a completely different source from those speculating at the time. The *Glasgow Observer*'s 'Man in the Know' columnist wrote an article in 1914 about the Celtic veterans, Welford and Doyle. In this article there is one little gem which harks back to that lost night. He was writing about Doyle's versatility as a sportsman, billiards being a game at which he excelled. 'Man in the Know' wrote:

> I have seen Doyle take on a few who fancied themselves with the cue, and none of us who saw him handle a young and ambitious journalist in a billiard room in Liverpool on the eve of the international of 1895 will ever forget the consternation of the youngster when, after giving the Celt a start and receiving a walloping, he took the same start and was beaten by an even bigger margin at the second attempt.

Players having a night on the town before a big game was no big deal to newspapermen or to clubs either in those days. A Friday night at the dancing was the norm for a lot of young players for a very long time. Whether Doyle was indeed physically fit to play in the game itself, which took place on 6 April, was probably answered by the fact that although the team was comprehensively defeated 3–0, the back division was deemed the most sound of the lot, both backs performing like Trojans, each of them stalling the England attack time and time again.

Doyle, despite the anxiety and apprehension of his pre-match behaviour, played 'splendidly with a nerve and accuracy that was gratifying to watch' (*Scottish Sport*, 9 April 1895). Drummond and Doyle were regarded as a line that could not be improved upon. Scotland had a goal struck off for off-side, with

England scoring almost immediately after from a mysterious free kick, and it was generally felt that the refereeing went from bad to worse, with even the crowd letting their feelings be known.

Although the England goalkeeper Sutcliffe had three times as much work to do as McArthur, the Scottish forwards were badly let down by the halfbacks. The team, though, at no time gave up, which was some consolation for the supporters who'd travelled down to cheer their team on. This game reopened the old argument as to whether or not Scotland should play Anglos. The tradition had been to choose only home-based Scots but, in doing this, Scotland had lost the chance to play many of her finest players over the previous twenty years.

Doyle was selected for the Scottish League team against the Football League for the match to be played in Glasgow and, although he had a continuing recovery of form, the team went down 1–4, Doyle redeeming himself in the eyes of the supporters and of the selectors alike. He'd obviously been tarred with the same brush as the rest of the team defeated at Goodison Park as some people had blamed more than the halfbacks for the defeat.

The reverberations of that International continued into 1896 and, for the first time, Anglos were selected for the International trials but in a different format. It was, in fact, a departure from the norm as this was Home-Scots versus Anglo-Scots, the Home-Scots having no fewer than seven Celts in the team, with the usual trials comprising solely of Home-Scots coming up later in the month. Up until then, only home-based

Scots were eligible for selection and the defeat at Goodison Park had finally made the selectors realise that, in ignoring the others, they were and always had been severely restricting their pool of eligible players.

According to *Scottish Sport,* this team was chosen to test the ability and mettle of the Anglo-Scots. A Liverpool newspaper reported that, during the course of a chat with some prominent Celts (Doyle was invariably termed 'a prominent Celt' when the reporter did not wish to name him directly), he was informed that they keenly felt they were being 'had' over this particular game. They felt that the Home team should have been more representative, with all the best home players taking part in order to field the strongest team available.

It had once been mooted that fielding the entire Celtic team against England was the only sure way to win but this was not a serious suggestion. If, at first, fielding seven of the Celtic team against the Anglos had looked like a compliment to Celtic, the players saw it differently. They were convinced that they had been chosen so that, if they didn't shine against the Anglos, who would be playing for all they were worth, it would be a good excuse to drop them when it came to picking the International side. Whether or not their suspicions were correct, the fact was that eventually only one Celt was in fact picked for the International side to face England.

The two trial teams met in March and Doyle was regarded as being a pale shadow of himself, with *Scottish Sport*'s writer in March 1896 adding that it would be 'criminal' to select him. He was also jeered very badly by the crowd and it was considered that this had an adverse effect on his play. Dan also didn't take too kindly to being cautioned by the referee so, all things considered, he was not having a nice day. The writer also didn't like Doyle's team-mate Meehan and he thought Kelly's placing to be extremely ill-timed, judging him to be too old 'to regain the art'. He regarded Ferguson as never being dangerous and believed Madden's good work was negated by his love of tripping and taking questionable 'disadvantage of an opponent'. So none of the Celts was having a nice day!

Despite all this, the general feeling was that the Home players were as good as any of the Anglos. But the Anglos managed to get their tuppence worth of opinion in as well, stating that the team they faced was 'too much Celtic'. It was, however, said that there was too much disparagement of Doyle's play at this time and that there seemed to be a general dead set against him.

In April 1896, the Scottish League team suffered an unexpected defeat, being routed 5–1 at Goodison Park. Doyle as usual had got a wonderful reception from the crowd, still being a great favourite there. It was generally agreed that the Scots had a much better team but the stronger won the game. Although Doyle was not in his best form, he did a vast amount of recovery work, using both his head and his feet, and he was especially effective at close quarters. The outcome of this particular game was that Scotland saw she had to revise the way the team played and one newspaper suggested that in future, when Drummond captained the team, his instructions to the players should be changed from 'Lie furrit, forwards!' to 'Gang furrit!'

In 1897, Doyle put in a sterling performance in the trials and all agreed that he hadn't a peer in that position and so Doyle no doubt had high hopes of his cap against England. This particular game at the Crystal Palace proved to be the only time he was on the winning side against them. The native sports writers were more than satisfied with the fitness of the team, commenting on the 'earnest diligence with which they have attended to their preparations'. They were also very impressed by SFA secretary Mr McDowall's timetable and one, *Scottish Sport*, published it in full on 2 April 1897:

Friday:

1.20pm; Train leaves St Enoch Station (Dining Saloons)

2pm; Luncheon

6.30pm; Dinner

10.45pm; Arrive in London. Buses waiting. Drive to Covent Garden Hotel

[In fact the team spent the night at Norwood, the Covent Garden being too noisy with fans for them to get any sleep.]

11.30pm; Supper

Saturday:

9am; Breakfast

12.40pm; Drive to Victoria Station to catch 1.10pm train to Crystal Palace

1.46pm; arrive at Crystal Palace

2pm; Luncheon in garden hall

4pm; kick-off [England defeated 1–2 only the England goalkeeper keeping the Scotland victory to a single goal]

6.30pm; Dinner in garden hall

7.38pm; Leave Crystal Palace for London

8.14pm; Arrive at Victoria Station

11.30; Supper

Sunday:

10am; Breakfast

11am; Leave for Zoological Gardens [where Doyle reputedly mistook polar bears for pigs!]

5pm; Dinner in Covent Garden Hotel

8pm; Tea

8.30pm; Buses leave Covent Garden Hotel for St Pancras

9.15pm; Leave St Pancras for Glasgow

Monday:

7.10am; Arrive at St Enoch Station

7.30am; Breakfast in City Restaurant

An impressive, if optimistic, timetable indeed!

English reporters saw the game as potentially one of physique versus speed. J. J. Bentley, writing in *Sporting Chronicle*, suggested that George Allan of Liverpool might be refused permission to play in the game by his club for contravening orders not to remain behind in

Sheffield after the inter-city game. He had been seen there, dallying in the company of a well-known Celt. Wonder who that was! It was rumoured that Allan, Scotland's centre for the Crystal Palace game, was due at Parkhead the following season. There had been talk of Doyle being an 'extinct volcano' but it was suggested that this opinion came from those who hadn't seen him play of late and were basing this judgement more on Celtic's defeats than on Doyle's part in them. However, the advice given to Smith, the right back for Scotland, was that he should be less impetuous and not leave it to the slower Doyle to catch the fast English sprinters.

The game itself, played on 3 April, was described in *The Times* as 'a fine exhibition of good football' that was played throughout at a fast pace, with Scotland achieving a brilliant victory. Their reporter also attributed victory to the power of the fullbacks and the halfback trio. England took the lead halfway through the first half, with a goal from Bloomer, but Hyslop equalised for Scotland five minutes later in a scramble following a free kick. Although Scotland's forwards were showing better understanding than the English and their speed was too much for the opposing backs, the winner eluded them until seven minutes from time when Miller's shot put the Scottish fans and team into ecstasy.

There had been a close call for Scotland when England had almost been gifted a goal by Patrick, the Scotland goalkeeper, running out and getting in Doyle's way as he was clearing the ball. But that was forgotten when the final whistle sounded. The ever-present *Scottish Sport*'s man was there and, on 6 April 1897, he recorded that 'whenever the referee sounded "Time", the Scotsmen raised a hair-raising yell and, as the spectators filed out of the vast enclosure, they were treated to astonishing Highland reels by exuberant Scotsmen to the doubtful music of miniature bagpipes'.

It had been a hard, dour struggle, apparently, and the celebrations at the Covent Garden Hotel must have been something else for even the garrulous reporters kept silent about what went on (or couldn't remember!) and referred any such enquiries to those they deemed best qualified to tell the tale – the workmen and employees of the hotel. One rumour did come out during the celebrations – that Doyle and Lambie both admitted having deliberately handled the ball inside the twelve-yard line within minutes of each other. Whether it was true – and no English protest was heard concerning those dastardly deeds – or it was the whisky talking, no one knows. It was said of this game that Lambie captained the team but Doyle bossed it.

Fresh from the great result at the Crystal Palace, Doyle took his place in the line-up for the Scottish League team versus the Football League at Ibrox Park. Not one person thought the team worth backing as it was considered a feeble and ill-assorted eleven and so its complete drubbing of the opposition was something of a sensation, the defence, it seems, playing to perfection. According to *Scottish Sport*, 6 April 1897, Smith and Doyle stood up to their opponents in 'faultless fashion and were a good few feet above their contemporaries on the English side'.

During the match, it was evident that Nick Smith, who had been elected captain, had apparently decided to let Doyle take his place or, if he hadn't, Dan did it just the same and did it in great style. The Scottish team won 3–0 and, with a little luck in the first half, it could have been more. Doyle, who was an extremely accurate kicker of the ball, did what he had done on many occasions in his career and put the ball directly into the net from a free kick. This was not allowed in those days, as the ball had to be touched first by another player, and the goal didn't stand. Although the forwards were a bit suspect in this game, they got their goals by sheer dint of perseverance and grit. *Scottish Sport* reported on 27 April that 'Doyle's fine generalship was all that was wanted to make undoubtedly what we possessed, a powerful combination'.

An electrifying display had been expected from the English forwards but, unfortunately for their team, they did not play to form. This wasn't too great a disappointment for the forty thousand spectators at Ibrox that day as they were more than happy with the performance of their own team.

The last game against England in which Doyle represented Scotland was, fittingly enough, played at Celtic Park in April 1898. The debate as to which players would be selected for the backs centred round Doyle and Drummond – the comment being made that the English forwards would prefer facing Rangers' Drummond to Celtic's Doyle. As it turned out, both were selected, with Dan being given his preferred position of left back.

But, before this, he had to face Ireland in Belfast where the Scots would win 3–0. This trip was voted one of the best ever, with only an assault on the referee by a disgruntled Irish supporter as he went into the pavilion at full-time marring the proceedings. Although the referee pointed out his assailant to one of the officials and asked to have the culprit arrested, the official declined to do anything about it. The Irish League determined to make a searching inquiry into it and, on 29 March 1898, *Scottish Sport* labelled it 'a disgrace to Irish football'.

Mr J. Reid, secretary of the Irish FA, said he hoped Scotland would beat England the following Saturday but didn't actually think they would. He was coming to Celtic Park anyway with all the Irish players, who'd been given free tickets for the match, to lend his support in case it was required. At the dinner after-wards, one of the SFA committee managed to speak for sixty minutes 'in a brogue he'd acquired as the vessel neared Ireland' (*Scottish Sport,* 29 March 1898). The team were given an even noisier send-off at Belfast than usual and it was suggested that some of the vocalists would have been better off in their beds.

Apparently, on the Thursday night, aboard *The Dromedary,* the ferry taking them to Belfast, the team had met the old Celt Mick McKeown and he was having a bit of a rough time. Mick had been the brilliant player Doyle had replaced at Celtic in 1891. A great deal of speculation had taken place during the trip regarding the composition of the team to face England, the joke being that Doyle had ordered six suits of clothes, forty barrels of oil, forty-five barrels of beer and unlimited whisky and he had also placed orders for half-a-dozen full-page adverts as sweeteners for the selectors to secure his cap for the game against England!

A good deal of entertainment was provided for the team on the Friday. They were put up at the Imperial Hotel in Belfast itself where nothing was too much trouble for all the staff. On the Friday morning, there was a drive to Bangor and then an evening visit to the Empire Palace. Saturday morning saw them having a general drive around Belfast and, in the evening, there was great rejoicing at the result of the game and a fireworks display. The teams did not socialise after the game and the Scots were left to dine alone at the banquet. The Scottish players each received a bottle of whiskey and a glass from Dunville and Co., a pocketknife from Lipsey and Co. and a badge from a local businessman – no wonder it was voted one of the best-natured trips ever.

On 2 April, Scotland met England at Parkhead and, in front of a crowd of forty thousand, went down 3–1. The game was rated one of the poorest shows by a Scottish International team – a complete reversal of the previous year. The first goal set the tone. As Spikesley of Sheffield Wednesday tore down on the Scots' goal, the Scottish backs both rushed out to cover. Drummond, getting hold of the ball at a bad angle, only succeeded in putting it in front of his own goal. It went up in the air and Charlie Athersmith, the England inside left, got to it and passed to Whelden who scored. At half-time, England were two goals up.

When play resumed, the Scottish wingers switched places and the best Scottish attacking moves came about, resulting in a fine goal from Miller. But the final nail in the coffin came when England scored a hotly disputed third, with all Scottish protests for offside being summarily dismissed by the referee. The England victory was attributed to its halfback line keeping the Scots forwards in check.

The newspapers reported that the crowd were puzzled by the strange play of Aston Villa's Cowan, the Scottish centre half, who had evidently failed continually at what he was supposed to do and went off 'in a series of eccentric dribbles', invariably losing the ball. This, according to one of the players, had a very disheartening effect on the team, as can well be imagined. Before the game, the committee, suspecting something was wrong, had asked James Cowan if he was fit to play. Cowan explained he had a cold and, although a reserve had already begun to strip, Cowan was allowed to take his place in the team. Cowan had been expected to be the mainstay of the team but evidently he hadn't been on the field ten minutes when it became apparent to everybody that there was something seriously wrong and, before twenty minutes had elapsed, the crowd were hissing their fallen idol.

The result of all this was that, at an SFA meeting the following Tuesday, there was an attempted vote of 'no confidence' in the selection committee. Cowan was defended by Mr J. Campbell-Orr of the Birmingham FA who'd spoken to the player both before and after the game and found him to be perfectly sound. Nothing more was heard of the matter but Cowan never again played for Scotland and there were no Anglos in the next side that faced England except for John Bell who had, in the meantime, transferred to Celtic. The unfortunate part, of course, was that Cowan was, in fact, the Scotland captain that fateful day!

As for Doyle, the failure was generally agreed to have lain at various players' feet but certainly not at the back, where both he and Drummond were said to have acquitted themselves well. *Scottish Sport* reported, on 5 April 1898, that Doyle and Drummond were, in the heroic language of the day, playing:

> with a broken shield in front of them and they emerged from this rather severe burden with great credit. They were seldom beaten and they succeeded in relegating the England outside 'fliers' to a relatively subordinate position. England's destructive power came from the inside trio and should have been dealt with before they reached the lengths of Doyle and Drummond.

Doyle, it was said, 'emerged from the field laden with honours but these were of the type that people bestow on the leader of a forlorn hope'. But Doyle was not the official leader! Scotland's second-half play only served to show what might have been if the radical weakness in a most important position hadn't prevented this happening.

Daniel Doyle finished his International career playing for the Scottish League against the Irish League at Cliftonville, Belfast, in February 1899. His selection no doubt surprised Dan as much as it did everyone else as he'd only played for Celtic on a handful of occasions that season, his career winding down now that he was in his thirty-fifth year. But Scottish Cup ties had a hand in the availability of players for selection and Doyle was nominated for the left-back slot, finding himself in the same team as another two of his Celtic mates, Sandy McMahon and Barney Battles, and so Dan, no doubt, was as pleased as Punch that he was set to go on another 'jolly boys outing'.

His selection had caused the usual ripples, this time quite understandably, but it was acknowledged that he could be relied on to do his very best. Also, he was always able to turn on the style in representative matches and, even if he didn't, his presence and leadership qualities were worth the selection itself. The Irish team was reckoned to be a very good one and a fine game was expected. It is interesting to note that, before the Ireland International of 1898, one of the Scottish players, Thomson, had received a letter from two Irish 'well-wishers' warning him about Peden, a left-winger who had no equal in the dirty-play department. Peden, who had played for Newton Heath (later to become Manchester United), before returning to Ireland, had now been selected to play for the Irish League team in 1899.

Throughout the game, the Scots were subjected to the roughest play they'd ever encountered, Peden being the worst offender by a mile. Not even the referee, a Belfast man, escaped his tongue-lashing and that's saying something for this particular referee jumped his own height when Ireland scored. No way to treat your friends! It was later suggested that a local man was not the right person to referee such matches.

Peden was not sent off for this offence against the referee nor, indeed, for any other of the blatant misdemeanours he committed.

At one point, Doyle was attacked from the rear by Mercer and it was clear that the referee had seen the incident. *Scottish Sport*, on 14 February 1899, said that Doyle's face was a 'beautiful study as he looked back over his shoulder of surprise mingled with something of why-didn't-you-do-it-harder'. The same paper also reported that the referee was generally regarded as a 'failure with a capital F' and the Scots received no protection from him whatsoever. At one point, Celtic's Barney Battles fell winded but play still went on. An unnamed Scot tackled the referee about this.

> Player: How the blank didn't you blow your whistle when you saw one of our men knocked out?
>
> Referee: How the blank didn't he say he was knocked out?
>
> Player: You blank blank of a blankety blank, how the blank could he?

The player was then threatened with being reported to the authorities.

Thanks to the referee and a superb Irish goalkeeper, the Scottish team lost 3–1 but Doyle had reportedly been as resourceful as ever and he could still give the younger men a run for their money. Apparently, an Irish spectator declared the Scottish team the roughest that had ever come to Ireland. The newspapermen thought this a terrible injustice to Peden!

At the dinner afterwards in the International Restaurant, all sat down to a beautiful meal purveyed by local Irish caterers, Messrs McGlade. It was reckoned to be as fine a dinner as footballers had ever partaken of and, out of compliment to the occasion, they were also entertained to champagne, cigars and cigarettes. But, despite this, the poor display of refereeing was not forgotten by the players who had been put at risk and, before the dinner, the Scottish team held an informal meeting where they agreed on a plan to show their disapproval of the referee. The original proposal was watered down somewhat and they agreed on the action they did indeed take to make their protest known. When the toast proposing the referee's health took place, they all rose and left the room. It was considered 'bad form' but it was also acknowledged that they had been sorely tried. The outcome of it all gave the players some satisfaction for the Scottish League decided that they would insist on two things at the next encounter – namely that the referee be neutral and that Peden be not selected.

Thus ended Dan Doyle's international career but both he and his old friend McMahon of Celtic, who'd also been a member of the Scottish League team, had decided that they could have a second career together. During their trip to Belfast, they had seen a man at the Empire Theatre telling tall stories about the Klondyke and Doyle and McMahon reckoned they could do even better with magic lantern scenes of the steerage life they had endured during their trips to Ireland in the service of their country.

9

A Different Arena

Even before his career had finally finished, Doyle was casting his eye about for new outlets for his overabundance of restless energy as he recognised that, soon, playing football would no longer be an option and the great wind-up of directors and press would be lost to him forever. By late 1898, he was thirty-four years old and, in the game of that period, it was a very exceptional man indeed who could have withstood the acute physical punishment that went with playing top-class football and come out the other side unharmed. Doyle had never spared himself. He had always been in the thick of the action, never shirking and probably giving more than he got – as one or two English international wingers could testify. Of course, he had his pubs and, despite the official Celtic denial that they had acquired it for him, he also owned the Drill Hall, the hub of Mossend–Bellshill social life. That ever-generous Celtic-supporting fairy godfather!

Scottish Sport said, 'We are requested to give a contradiction to the statement that the Celtic have

bought, on behalf of Doyle, the property in which his business is situated.' This came a day or so after he'd re-signed in May 1894 despite Everton, at the same time, offering to establish him as proprietor of his favourite pub in Liverpool with a lease extending over nineteen years and £5 a week in return for signing for two years. Whether or not Doyle ever meant to leave Celtic, we'll never know, but he had met and talked with Mr Molyneux of Everton in April of that year and they were obviously on very friendly terms. Doyle was in Liverpool with the Scottish League team for the match against the Football League and had received the warmest of welcomes from the Liverpudlians both at the start and at half-time. He obviously used this approach by Everton as a bargaining tool with Celtic during his re-signing talks.

Doyle felt great kinship with the firebrands of the day and, with his suspect temper on the field liable to break out at any moment, they, no doubt, had much in common with Dan. However, excluding the Stoke game, where he knew he couldn't be punished, he was only ordered off once in his career and this must bear testimony to the fact that he was more than able to keep his temper when he wanted to. During a game against Dundee, he was given a rough time by a young player but the news reports stated that, despite this, Dan didn't once lose his temper, which seemed to surprise them. This was probably because some of his greatest fans could be numbered among the Dundee Irish and Dan was not out to offend them by teaching the youngster a rather severe lesson.

So it was that, in late 1898, Dan Doyle declared his candidacy for the Bellshill Parish Council. Evidently being a member of the Bellshill and Mossend Wine and Beer Association was not enough to satisfy Dan's new-found craving for public do-goodery. This was the new Dan, Bellshill's social conscience, and, as the journalist of *Scottish Sport* in the edition of 23 December 1898 suggested, 'Doyle is sure to be made chairman of the Finance Committee sooner or later'. This was in reference to an old 'linesman or Chancellor' quip when Doyle had once remarked, in an interview in *Scottish Sport*, 24 May 1895, that, when he retired, he'd either become a linesman or the Chancellor of the Exchequer. Doyle, incidentally, was frequently Celtic's linesman and was an excellent one at that, being much admired for his speed and sureness in decision-making.

He had a hard time at the 'hustings' where severe heckling was the order of the day but he managed it with aplomb for, as always, Doyle was supremely pragmatic when it suited him. He fielded the soul-searching questions from his fellow-citizens with ease. Their obvious concern with the major issues of the day could be seen in questions such as: Who do you regard as the best left-back in Britain?; What do you think of the league transfer system?; and, when the local intellectual got a word in, Are you in favour of an eight-hour day in all trades? The last one was hardly something that would be within the remit of the parish councillor!

The *Bellshill Speaker* recorded the votes given to each candidate. The top seven would be elected and Doyle was returned seventh. The newspaper remarked that:

Mr Doyle seems not only to have got the solid Catholic vote but a fair amount of support from the Protestant community. We do not think he deserved this, seeing the policy of the party was to vote one and throw away the other six …. We regret that Mr Urquhart did not receive sufficient votes to win him seventh place.

Shortly afterwards, Dan probably regretted it too as he became a member, not of the finance committee but of the cemetery one. Needless to say, Doyle's first flush of enthusiasm soon died a death and he went absent – no apology ever being given – for some eight months after attending the first few meetings of the council and thus set the pattern for future attendances. Being Mr Social Conscience of the People, who had in no way altered his own behaviour, did not give him the same thrill as being 'Celtic's Great and Only Dan'. How to calculate the necessary trajectory of a football instantly was immensely more his forte than surmising how many gravediggers were required when there was a rush on!

Doyle had a driving need to be top dog but he'd now entered a world where the skills required no longer included the best of his footballing ones and, in addition, he did not have the basic interest in what he was doing to compete in the mind-numbing tedium of local politics. The writing was on the wall and Doyle allowed himself unwittingly to become the victim of terminal boredom in a world where his fiercely competitive spirit would be subsumed in the drawn-out war of attrition that was local politics. His greatest assets were neither appreciated nor required.

Sport and gambling had always been Doyle's greatest interests in life. The miners' love of quoiting had been heartily embraced by him most successfully since his youth. This sport required great strength, skill and stamina. During the Everton–Celtic battle for his services in 1891, Doyle had finally eluded the Everton directors by assuring them he was just going to Scotland to take part in a quoiting handicap which he thought he stood a fair chance of winning. Perhaps if they'd known that one of the main quoiting grounds was at Camlachie, half a mile from Celtic Park, they'd have waved him off with less goodwill. Big money was involved at these events, prizes of up to £50 could change hands and, coupled with gambling being the order of the day, it was a sport that was tailor-made for Doyle.

Sadly, though, it was during one of these events many years later that Doyle, who was in his fifties by this time and throwing just for old times' sake at Kirkintilloch, sustained an injury to his neck which required medical treatment as the pain was so severe. It was while he was undergoing this treatment that it was discovered that he was suffering from a terminal illness.

Quoiting was really a young man's game and Doyle wisely concentrated on another miners' favourite, bowls. In 1903, the great Dr W. G. Grace, the icon of English cricket and also a keen bowler, organised the first England v Scotland international bowling match at the Crystal Palace to be played under the Scottish Bowling Association rules. Doyle was selected to play for his country and the trip probably brought back old memories of his days of travelling round the country and over the Border as he'd done frequently when playing for Celtic and Scotland.

This time, though, there were no Maddens, Reynoldses or Campbells to keep the wayward lad of old company or to linger behind with him for a while. There was also no danger of a bowling team being refused entry to a hotel because of their reputation for rowdiness – although Willie Maley maintained that the club was always more than willing to pay for the damage done as a result of these 'high jinks'.

The game was drawn but England, having had more throws, was declared the winner. The match in July 1903 was reported in the *Bellshill Speaker* but, strangely enough, no mention was made of Doyle, a leading light in the local Bellshill and Mossend Bowling Club.

But football remained a part of his life and he became president of Mossend Hibs and, when required, was happy to help out refereeing schoolboy charity matches. Jimmy Quinn's testimonial took place in 1907 and the complete list of contributors was published in the *Glasgow Star*. Many of the old players were in the packed St Mungo's Halls in Glasgow for the main event but Doyle wasn't one of them. Yet his name is on the list of subscribers. Daniel Doyle of Bellshill – one guinea. It was one of the largest individual donations. The entire Celtic squad only gave eight guineas so it was a handsome gift indeed. Strangely enough, at the funerals of prominent Celtic directors, his name is always absent from the list of players present although men he'd played with are there, but he was usually present at those of his team-mates.

Doyle, variously described as always light-hearted and happy-go-lucky, was in fact a very complex man. How much his need to go against those in authority, no matter how affable the contest might be, had its origins in having been singled out to be separated from the rest of his family throughout his childhood and youth, is hard to tell.

His brother James, probably the one who played for a Paisley junior team, had been best man at Doyle's wedding in January 1894. He married Margaret Devlin, a colliery contractor's daughter. By 1902, James was also living in Doyle's house in Main Street, Bellshill, where Doyle's Horse Shoe Bar was situated. In March and April of that year, one week apart, both James's infant son Allan and then James himself died. Dan Doyle registered his brother's death. This must have been a massive blow as another of James's sons, three-year-old Daniel, had died in September of the previous year.

Cecilia Doyle, who had virtually been a mother to Doyle throughout his life, had died on 4 April 1898, two days after Doyle had represented Scotland against England at Celtic Park and a week before he captained the Scottish League team that played against the Football League at Birmingham. Another personal blow was the death in Doyle's house of John Doyle, the cousin he'd grown up with, and Dan registered this death too. I have been unable to find the births of any children born to Dan Doyle but that is not to say there weren't any.

In the book, *Alex James – Life of a Football Legend*, by John Harding, Alex James, a Mossend lad himself, is quoted as saying that Doyle didn't keep his pubs long as he hit the bottle and lost everything. In fact, Doyle had the licence for the Horse Shoe Bar for nineteen years and 'the conduct of the business had always been admirable' was the comment recorded in the Licensing Court. Admirable or not, even during his Celtic-playing days, Doyle was liable to be assaulted in the pub. Indeed, on 29 July 1899, a man was charged with having assaulted him in his pub on 25 December 1896 and he was fined twenty shillings or fourteen days. But Dan's assailant had immediately hopped it back to Ireland where he remained for several years. Retribution and Doyle were obviously waiting for him on his return. Who said Doyle never held a grudge?

Alex James attributes Doyle's downfall to drink and no doubt it played its part but it was certainly not the only cause. Doyle was the product of a hard-drinking community with a love of gambling and it was what made Doyle Doyle. Drink and gambling were part of Doyle's life from when he was a youngster and it was probable that, when one got out of control, the other became a refuge. The Bellshill of this period, especially Main Street where Doyle had his pub, was rife with illegal gambling and, according to the *Bellshill Speaker*, the authorities were hard-pressed to get it under control.

Doyle was an inveterate gambler all his life – it is likely he became addicted to it at an early age – and he would bet on the most trivial matter, his faithful companion being a double-tailed coin. One evening, on the way home to Bellshill, he suggested to the cab driver, whom he knew, that he would toss him double or quits for the fare. The cab driver agreed, called heads and duly lost. He then offered to toss for the cab and horse. With Dan having the right to call this time, he promptly won. He told the cabbie he would call round the following morning to pick up his winnings. The next day, he turned up, paid his fare and made a gift of 'his' horse and cab to the cabbie. Whether gambling – and there's no doubt he did some serious stuff – was another way of feeding that insatiable need for status now that the days of 'the one and only Dan' were gone, only Doyle would know.

There is no doubt that he eventually lost everything including his businesses but the facile story of his drinking leading to the loss is quite wrong. Had he been the hopeless drunk at this time. as was suggested, his business would not have been run as admirably as the police testified. By 1910, he had handed over the running of the pub. This was not because he was physically incapable of running the business but principally because he was financially insolvent. For a working-class lad to have been afforded such golden opportunities and to have thrown them away is deplorable to those of us who haven't had these chances. But any judgement of Doyle must be allied to an understanding of the man's nature which was one of both great needs and excesses. He had immense charm and used it mercilessly to get his own way – being in control was what life for Dan Doyle was all about.

However, he didn't throw away everything he had earned as was suggested. He had, in fact, helped slowly and systematically to destroy it himself, the greatest impact probably coming from his gambling.

Consequently, he lost that control which was so vital to his own mental well-being. There was probably no way Doyle could have been truly fulfilled once the high that he got from his playing days were gone. There was no way he was capable of finding a substitute and the miracle is that he tholed it as long as he did. There is something about the wonderful free spirit that was Doyle being locked into the soul-destroying boredom of the cemetery committee that is an affront to human nature.

Doyle was still being voted a director of Bellshill and Mossend Bowling Club as late as 1909 and was obviously still a respected member of the community, not a drunken ex-businessman. The final nail in Doyle's business life was acted out in the Licensing Court in 1911. The first real hint of trouble came with the announcement in the *Bellshill Speaker* that the Drill Hall had been sold to an Orange lodge in 1909.

Doyle was, by this time, greatly in need of money to pay off his debts. On 12 May 1911, it was reported in the *Bellshill Speaker* that Dan Doyle's appeal to have his licence for the Horse Shoe Bar restored had been dismissed. The original application to transfer the licence to a Glasgow man or renew it in Doyle's name had not only been refused but the licence for that particular public house had been taken away altogether on the grounds of congestion. At that time, there was one licence for every one hundred and forty-four of the population of the immediate area.

It then transpired that the licence had virtually been transferred on a private basis and Doyle hadn't set foot in it for over a year, having been paid £2 a week to keep out. Consequently, the police declared they couldn't accept him as the tenant. When asked why the unofficial transfer had taken place, the reply was 'financial difficulties' with 'and others' added on. The fiscal was somewhat riled that the business had been a brewer's house for some considerable time without the Licensing Court having been informed. It was denied that the licence was wholly in the hands of the brewer as there were other creditors as well. Dan was obviously in dire financial straits. The appeal was dismissed and Doyle's licence was not renewed on the extremely unfair grounds of congestion. Doyle's and two other cases brought at the same sitting in May were used by the *Glasgow Herald* that year to illustrate the arbitrary nature of refusing licences and the injustice done to the individuals involved.

Thus Dan Doyle lost any means he had of attempting to repay his debts through his public house or even simply trying to earn a living. Although he was most probably the architect of his own financial plight, Doyle was also to some extent a victim of circumstances.

So Doyle, completely down on his luck, migrated back to the scene of his greatest days, Glasgow's East End. His haunts were now firmly based around Celtic Park where, as a Celtic great, his company was always sought after in the favourite pubs and gathering places of the supporters – more so than a failed businessman's would have been in Bellshill. Again the myth is that he went there as a down-and-out. Doyle, in fact, was given a job in an engineering factory by Tom Robertson, the famous referee and future president of the Scottish League.

Perhaps it's significant that the man who declared in 1892, when he had acquired his first pub, that, in future, he'd be known as Dan Doyle of Bellshill, was noted in his death notice in the *Glasgow Observer* as being late of Celtic FC and Mossend. Doyle was still a favourite with newspapermen who valued his shrewd opinions of players both past and present and he never lost their admiration. Of material possessions he had very little but his mind still held a wealth of football experience and sound judgement equal to none and the sportswriters knew it. No doubt the East End held the added attraction for him of the presence of his staunch friend and team-mate in the Celtic defence, Jerry Reynolds, who was, by this time, an odd-job man and gateman at Celtic Park. Doyle had always loved to reminisce with old friends and Reynolds was very entertaining company in his own inimitable style.

Willie Maley tells in his own reminiscences that it was he who got Tom Robertson to give Doyle the job in his engineering works. Perhaps both Robertson and Doyle remembered with a smile the evening in December 1895 when, along with Mr Mearchant, the vice-president of Queen's Park, that they'd been the judging committee of the 'Comic Singers Competition' at Greenock Town Hall or the time when Doyle had let rip at Robertson for having the nerve to caution him for rough play during the Home versus Anglos match.

There is no doubt Willie Maley was a good friend to Doyle when he was sorely in need of one and that is the true judge of a man's character. Maley, who proclaimed Doyle to be one of his heroes, stood to gain nothing except perhaps the joy of talking football with a man who'd also lived through most of that first roller-coaster decade in Celtic's history and who had, undoubtedly, given the committee – and then Maley himself – most of their managerial headaches.

However, the inspirational Doyle had been the catalyst in the massive upsurge in the crowds going through the gates at Parkhead – for skill is something universally appreciated by football fans – but skill allied to an irreverent wildness is, and always will be, irresistible to the Celtic support.

10

Evergreen

Dan Doyle died on 8 April 1918 at the age of fifty-three in the Glasgow Cancer Hospital of cancer of the throat and cervical glands. This was nineteen years after he'd retired from Celtic and professional football. Doyle was 'the sagest of coaches' (*Glasgow Observer*, 5 June 1897) in his playing days and one wonders why he didn't follow the example of his great friend and team-mate, Johnny Madden, the so-called 'father of Czech football', into that side of the game. Perhaps his powerful and dominant personality rang warning bells with committeemen throughout the land who reckoned that the last thing they wanted was an employee who needed no courses in self-assertiveness!

In August 1899, at a meeting of the SFA, a committee member asked if Doyle's name was among those who'd been reinstated as an amateur. When it was confirmed that it was, 'the member seemed pleased and smiled a smile that gradually wormed its way round the table'. The feelings of relief are almost palpable when reading that report. That he had caused temporary shivers of anxiety among the powers that be at that meeting would have raised a smile from Doyle had he known it – it would also have caused the Celtic support to cheer their bould bhoy loudly.

In the Bellshill area today, there are several Celtic Supporters Clubs but none is dedicated to the man who was the most celebrated Celt of his day.

It is often written that Willie Maley had a rough time trying to manage players such as Doyle who were of his own generation. He was, in fact, almost four years younger than Doyle and it's interesting to note that the players who caused him most bother as renegades, including Tommy McInally of later years, also gained his affection. Perhaps Maley, like most of us who come to heel more readily, had a sneaking regard for those who habitually kicked over the traces. The heavy hand was counter-productive with this kind of player so perhaps, in Maley's reluctantly accommodating style at that time, he had inadvertently stumbled upon the only way of working with the free spirit that was Doyle – for Dan always walked to the rhythm of his own drum and it would probably have been useless to try to change him.

Besides, it was partly this cavalier attitude to officialdom that so endeared him to the huge Celtic faithful and considerably boosted the takings at the gate. Celtic with Doyle was, for the most part, an infinitely superior team to Celtic without him and in that simple statement lies part, if not all, of the answer as to why strong-minded men like J. H. McLaughlin allowed him to do as he pleased. It is interesting to note how hard the Everton directors tried for years to recover the 'wandering soul' from Celtic despite knowing the problems he would be likely to pose them. The Celtic directors of 1897 – now answerable to shareholders – managed to face him down but that was when his career was in its twilight years.

Dan Doyle's funeral took place on 10 April 1918 and he was buried in St Peter's, Dalbeth, Glasgow, a mere stone's throw from Celtic Park and beside the future training ground of Barrowfield. The *Glasgow Observer* reported it thus:

> A representative football company attended the funeral of Dan Doyle on Wednesday. Among those who watched the remains of the great Celt being laid to rest were: Rev. Father Unsworth, SJ; Mrs Doyle; Messrs James Kelly and M. Dunbar of the Parkhead Board of Directors; W. Maley, the Celtic manager; Mr J. K. McDowall, Sec. of the SFA; Mr Tom Robertson (Q.P.), the well-known referee; Andrew Hannah, Doyle's colleague of the Everton defence; old Celtic favourites Jerry Reynolds, Jim Welford, John Campbell and Willie Loney; James McMenemy of the present day team; and Messrs Dan Morgan (Renfrewshire), Tom Pate (Kirkintilloch) and George Moore (Glasgow).

> Wreaths were sent by the Celtic FC, by the present-day players at Parkhead, by the players who sported the 'green and white' in Dan's time and by the Hibernian FC.

There is a feel about it that causes one to see Willie Maley's hand in the list of those present. Doyle is noted in the records of the Archdiocese of Glasgow which owns the cemetery as a friend of the lair owner, not as either the owner or a family member. Had he died ten years or so earlier, his funeral would have rivalled that of his friend and team-mate Barney Battles in 1905, when two thousand followed the cortege and forty thousand lined the route to the same cemetery. That day, the coffin had been carried out of the Sacred Heart in Bridgeton by Doyle, Campbell, McMahon and Orr.

Perhaps Dan Doyle was rightly labelled on his wife Margaret's death certificate some thirty-six years later where his occupation was described as 'coal-miner' – not footballer, spirit-merchant or even electric crane-driver as it was on his own – for it was, indeed, this mining background that had shaped his attitude and thinking. It had taken the restless, stubborn, hot-tempered yet likeable youth who was Daniel Doyle and moulded him into the most charismatic and enigmatic player of his generation. Jock Stein, himself a former Lanarkshire miner, said there were no slackers and phoneys down the pit for they were soon sussed out and put out. In modern parlance, you had to be a team-player and Doyle was always that on the pitch. When the chips were down, he was invariably the hardest trier, giving everything he had to the cause and, for most of his career, that cause was Celtic's.

The flags that flew at half-mast over Celtic Park at the first home game after his funeral were a fitting tribute to that great player. One of the original aims of the founding fathers on that evening of 6 November 1887 when proposing the new club was to give the Irish in the West of Scotland a pride in their own identity. In the wild rover that was Dan Doyle, the Celtic faithful had a man who was the embodiment of their own hopes of rising above the mundane whilst remaining independent of soul. Tom Maley wrote that it was as a Celt Doyle cared to be known and it is as one of the greatest he will be forever remembered.

Bibliography

Books

Arnott, R. Page, *A History of the Scottish Miners*
Campbell, Tom and Pat Woods, *A Celtic A–Z*
Campbell, Tom and Pat Woods, *Dreams and Songs to Sing*
Craig, Jim, *A Lion Looks Back*
Crampsey, Bob, *The First 100 Years* [The League]
Dron, Robert, *The Coalfields of Scotland*
Eckberg, C. and S. Woodhead, *The Mariners*
Gallacher, Tom, *Scottish Catholics and the British Left*
Gibson, A. and W. Pickford, *Association Football and the Men who Made It, vol. 4*
Handley, James E., *The Celtic Story*
Handley, James E., *The Navvy in Scotland*
Harding, John, *Alex James – Life of a Football Legend*
Hayes, Dean, *Everton A–Z*
Hutton, Guthrie, *Miners from Kirkintilloch to Clackmannan, Stirling to Slamannan*
Hutton, Guthrie, *Scotland's Black Diamonds*
James, Brian, *England v Scotland*
Johnston, Frank (ed.), *The Football Encyclopaedia*
Keates, Thomas, *History of Everton Football Club*

Keevins, Hugh, *Celtic Greats*

Lamming, Douglas, *A Scottish Soccer Internationalists' Who's Who*

Lincoln, Bob, *Reminiscences of Grimsby Town FC 1879–1912*

Lugton, Alan, *The Making of Hibernian, Part 1*

MacDonald, Catriona M. M., *The Radical Thread*

Maley, Willie, *The Story of the Celtic*

Marshall, Stuart, *Celtic Football Legends, 1888–1938*

Martin, Gus, *The Broxburn Football Story*

McBride, E., M. O'Connor and G. Sheridan, *An Alphabet of the Celts*

McCarra, Kevin, *Scottish Football – A Pictorial History*

McColl, G. and G. Sheridan, *The Essential History of Celtic*

McNee, Gerald, *The Story of Celtic*

McRoberts, David (ed.), *Modern Scottish Catholicism 1878–1978*

Mitchell, Martin J., *The Irish in the West of Scotland 1797–1848*

Old International, *Twenty-five Years of Football*

Onslow, Tony, *Everton FC – The Men from the Hill Country*

Potter, David, *Our Bhoys Have Won the Cup*

Potter, David, *Willie Maley*

Scottish Football Association Annual 1892–93

The Football Handbook – Season 1903/04

Traynor, John C., *Celtic Official All-time Greats*

Triggs, Les, *Grimsby Town – A Complete Record 1878–1989*

Weir, John, *A History of Cowlairs Football Club 1876–1896*

Scottish Football – A Source Book
Wherry, David, *We Only Sing when We're Fishing –
 Grimsby Town History – 1878–2000*
Wilson, Brian, *Celtic – A Century with Honour*
Woods, Pat, *Celtic FC Facts and Figures*
Young, Percy, *A History of British Football*

Newspapers

Airdrie and Coatbridge Advertiser
Athletic News
Bellshill Speaker
Bothwell Advertiser
Catholic Herald
Clyde Shipping Gazette
Daily Record and Mail
Evening Express (Liverpool)
Evening Sentinel (Stoke)
Evening Times
Falkirk Herald
Field Sports
Football Weekly
Glasgow Eastern Standard
Glasgow Evening News
Glasgow Examiner
Glasgow Herald
Glasgow Observer
Glasgow Star
Greenock Telegraph
Grimsby News
Irish Independent Weekly
North British Daily Mail

North-East Lanark Gazette
Pastime
Scottish Referee
Scottish Sport
Scottish Umpire
Scottish Weekly Record
Sporting Chronicle
Sunday Mail
The Celtic View
The Scotsman
The Times
The Weekly News
Weekly Record Mail

Miscellaneous Sources

Airdrie Central Library/Archives
Broxburn FC – www.broxburnfc.co.uk
Celtic Park Visitor Centre
Census Returns 1841–1901, New Register House, Edinburgh
Grimsby Central Library
Mitchell Library, Glasgow
Motherwell Heritage Centre
National Football Museum, Preston
National Newspaper Library, Colinton
Paisley Central Library
Poor Law Applications, Airdrie, Glasgow and Paisley
Post Office Directories
Report on the Sanitary Conditions of the Labouring Population of Scotland, 1842
Scottish Football Museum, Hampden Park, Glasgow

Scottish Match Archive –
   www.scottishfa.co.uk/stats/index.htm
SFA Registration Books
SFA Minute Books
Slater's Trade Directories
Stoke-on-Trent Archive Service

Index

Doyle (née Devlin), Margaret
150, 160
Drummond, John 125, 128,
131, 136, 138, 140
Duff, Andrew 36, 39
Duff, Tom 34
Dunbar, Mick 17, 52, 55, 76,
159
Dunbar, Tom 88, 92, 99

E
Eaglesham (Abercorn FC) 79

F
Ferguson, John 89, 131
Ferrier, F. (Dundee FC) 93,
94
Foyers, Robert 115, 116,
125–27

G
Gallacher, Paddy 16, 47, 76,
99, 102
Geary, Fred 19
Glass, John 1, 2, 20, 35, 48,
55, 72, 73, 80, 84, 97, 118
Goodall, John 119, 160
Goudie, John 81, 82
Grace, Dr W. G. 148
Grant, James 76
Groves, Willie 7, 17, 66, 73,
114

H
Hannah, Andrew 8, 19, 22,
47, 96, 159
Hardie, J. Keir 11

Hendry (Dundee FC) 93,
95
Holt, John 19
Hyslop, Tom 134

J
James, Alex 150, 151
Johnstone, Jimmy 107
Johnstone, William (Third
Lanark FC) 89

K
Keillor, Sandy (Dundee FC)
95
Kelly, James 39, 7, 79, 80,
86, 89, 94, 117, 131, 159
King, Alex 89
Kirkwood, A. (Dykehead)
126
Kirkwood, Danny 19

L
Lambie, Willie 117, 120, 135
Latta, Alec 19
Loney, Willie 159
Longair, William 94, 95
Lundie, Jimmy 6, 18

M
Madden, Johnny 36, 37, 39,
40, 47, 52, 59, 61, 71,
79–81, 83, 98–101, 131,
149, 157
Maley, Tom 7, 18, 39, 69, 72,
86, 106, 161
Maley, Willie 18, 34, 39, 45,
47, 49, 54, 64, 65, 69, 84,